REEF MAKING

*Transforming Oceans
One Artificial Reef at a Time*

DAVID WALTER

Copyright ©2019, David Walter

ALL RIGHTS RESERVED.

No part of this publication may be reproduced, stored in a retrieval system, or transmitted in any form or by any means—electronic, mechanical, photo-copy, recording, or any other—except for brief quotation in reviews, without the prior permission of the author or publisher.

ISBN: 978-1-948638-43-2

PRINTED IN THE UNITED STATES OF AMERICA

Table of Contents

Preface v
Foreword vii

Chapter 1	The Beginning	1
Chapter 2	First Reef Zone	7
Chapter 3	Red Snapper	15
Chapter 4	First Commercial Reef Builder	19
Chapter 5	Private Reefs	27
Chapter 6	Public Reefs	33
Chapter 7	Trust	37
Chapter 8	Economy and Rules	45
Chapter 9	Coast Guard	51
Chapter 10	Car Dealer	63
Chapter 11	Ships	69
Chapter 12	More Ships	85
Chapter 13	Lots of Changes	93
Chapter 14	Hard Times	101
Chapter 15	NOAA	111
Chapter 16	Struggling to Survive	119
Chapter 17	New Reef Design and Florida	123
Chapter 18	Acceptable Reef	135
Chapter 19	Complex Reef	139
Chapter 20	Snorkeling Reef	147
Chapter 21	Super Reef	153
Chapter 22	Turtles	161
Chapter 23	Wave Attenuator	167
Chapter 24	The Future and Restoring the World's Fisheries	171

Preface

Alabama's artificial reef program is unique. Today, it stands alone as the world's largest single artificial reef zone, and it is certainly the most successful reef-building program. It was chiefly responsible for transforming the tiny, obscure Orange Beach community into the number-one fishing destination in the Gulf of Mexico. Despite its success, however, details of Alabama's artificial reef program are still largely unknown to the general public.

The program came into existence during the mid-1980s, during a rare occasion when the right people were in the right place at the right time. In the intervening years, most of the individuals who participated and witnessed this historical event passed on to another life. I am one of the few left who both witnessed and participated in this episode in Alabama's history, which played an important part in the development of the nation's fisheries. This is my account of how the artificial reef program came into existence, and the role I played in its history, from 1986 to 2019.

David Walter

Foreword

The northern Gulf of Mexico has no natural reef system like those found in the Florida Keys, Cancun, Belize and other tropical areas of the Gulf. For the most part, the northern Gulf has a flat, sandy, desert-like bottom practically devoid of visible sea life. Put something there, even a beer can, and life begins to appear. Within a year, the same sort of sea life that takes up residence on natural coral reefs begins to populate any artificial reef. The bigger the object, the more life it attracts and supports. In addition to algae, barnacles, soft corals and tiny marine animals, a reef is home to red snapper, triggerfish, grouper and many other species. All live and grow on and around the structure. All depend on the structure to provide food and protection.

The construction of artificial reefs off Alabama's Orange Beach coast probably started in the 1930s. I don't have factual data to support that claim, just stories passed down through generations. No one living today knows for sure. Back in those days, when pelagic fish (king mackerel, Spanish mackerel, Wahoo, mahi-mahi, etc.) migrated south for the winter, fishing effectively ended for those species until the next year. I've heard stories about some of the original settlers of Orange Beach, charter boat pioneers such as the Callaways and Walkers, dumping junk off their small boats close to shore. To plot

Reef Making

the location of the reef, they used land ranges such as sand dunes lined up with a particular tree, beach cottages, water towers, etc. Such efforts provided them enough bottom-dwelling fish (demersal fish) during winters to feed their families through the years of the Great Depression.

At some point during World War II, reef building apparently ceased — or at least the stories of those times don't touch on the subject. The government commandeered some local boats for various tasks and returned them to their owners with the thanks of a grateful nation. For instance, Roy Walker's charter boat, *Miss Kay*, was accorded a brass plaque noting her service.

A temporary halt to reef building in that era makes sense, given that the war effort required full attention. The demand for manpower would have drawn fishermen into various other endeavors, including working in the shipyards, military service and other war effort activities. Finally, reef building in that era might have seemed suspicious: Military regularly patrolled the beaches, and there were reports of German spies and shipwrecked German submarine crews landing near Gulf Shores.

After the war, in 1953, the State deployed 250 car bodies offshore for artificial reefs at the request of charter boat fishermen. In 1957, the State deployed an additional 1,500 automobiles. In 1959, the Mobile County Wildlife and Conservation Association sunk a dry dock. In 1974, the state sank five Liberty Ship hulls. All these sunken materials had to be marked with buoys to allow fishermen to find them, but keeping buoys onsite was troublesome. There might have been some private reef-building activity going on, but no other officially recorded reef endeavor took place until 1987, which is when the following account begins.

CHAPTER 1

The Beginning

In the 1970s and early 1980s, hardly anyone engaged in recreational fishing in Orange Beach considered red snapper a desirable fish to catch. The Gulf provided an abundance of pelagic fish for fishermen and any building of reefs by individuals was sporadic and undocumented. Pelagic fish — meaning mackerel, wahoo and assorted other summer visitors — swim and feed near the surface. Demersal species such as red snapper, triggerfish, grouper, etc., live on the sea bottom. Pelagic fish come and go with the seasons. Demersal fish are here year-round.

On the Gulf Coast of Alabama, there are three waterfront towns. Starting at the Florida line is Orange Beach. It has a navigable pass to the Gulf of Mexico ("Perdido Pass," also known as "Alabama Point"). Gulf Shores lies about eight miles west of Orange Beach. Gulf Shores' access to the Gulf is a narrow, shallow pass from Little Lagoon. Boats drafting over a foot must use caution, so it's not a practical outlet for offshore fishing vessels. Gulf Shores does have access to the Intracoastal Canal, but boats must travel 14 miles east or 20 miles west to access the Gulf. Dauphin Island lies a good distance away near the

Reef Making

western end of Alabama's 45 miles of coastline. It uses the Mobile Bay Ship Channel for access to the Gulf.

Alabama's early recreational fishing efforts were divided between Dauphin Island and Orange Beach. In the end, Orange Beach became the most popular fishing destination, not only because of the fishing, but also for aesthetic reasons such as water clarity, the quality of beaches and the availability of more land for development.

Historically, fishing has been Orange Beach's main industry, and it was the primary reason people were first attracted to the area. In those early years, fishing boats filled the marinas. Sightseeing on pontoon boats, skiing, cruising the inland waters and partying on Robinson Island were almost non-existent activities. Likewise, all the restaurants, traffic and numerous stores and shops of today were somewhere in the future.

First and foremost, there was fishing, and it was almost exclusively limited to trolling for pelagic species. Almost no one considered bottom fishing for red snapper — for two reasons. First, there were plenty of pelagic fish to catch and no harvest limits were in effect. Also, the difficulty of finding bottom structure to fish for demersal species quelled most interest in bottom fishing. There was an area of natural reefs between Pensacola and Orange Beach — a series of low-relief ledges — but it was out of sight of land and there were no sophisticated navigation electronics available to pinpoint locations offshore. Consequently, this area was seldom recreationally bottom fished.

Navigation devices have evolved over hundreds of years, from the primitive to the modern marvels we have today. As an example of the development in equipment used to navigate from point A to point B, consider how we might locate a local Walmart store using tools available for the task through the ages.

The Beginning

In ancient times, a sextant was employed to navigate by measuring distances between celestial bodies, but it could only determine longitude location (north-south). Until an accurate clock (**chronometer**) was developed to plot sunrise for the latitude, determining east-west locations was virtually impossible. However, with a clock, a very good sextant and an experienced hand in celestial navigation, you could get to within a couple of miles of Walmart.

Sextant.

Moving on to the 1940s, the Massachusetts Institute of Technology, at the behest of the government, developed Loran (Long Range Navigation) for supply convoy shipping during the war. At first, the new system had a range of about only 600 miles. In the 1950s, Loran-C with a range of 2,000 miles came into being, but wasn't affordable until the late 1970s and early 1980s.

Before the introduction of solid-state electronics, the first Loran receivers consisted of a 1.5-foot square box with a small TV screen that received signals from land-based towers. To use it, one would tune the receiver to an east-west tower and a blip would appear on the tiny screen. Using numbered dials, the user would then move a second blip over the first blip until they aligned perfectly. Then the user would read the dials and copy down a five-digit number. Next, a north-south tower would be acquired, and the first operation repeated. Consulting

Reef Making

Though not perfect, Loran A was a step up from other navigation tools.

a special map with a Loran grid on it, and applying the readout numbers, would get you to within a couple of blocks of Walmart.

As is the case with all useful technology, the Loran system improved over time. By the mid-1980s Loran receivers had become smaller, more affordable and easier to use. It provided a digital readout of both Loran numbers, which was accurate enough to get you to a parking place closest to the front door of Walmart.

In the early 1980s, Loran-C was quite expensive and not needed for trolling for pelagic fish inshore. Most boats only had a compass, a CB radio and perhaps a UHF (and later, a VHF) marine radio. If

The Beginning

they did possess a Loran machine, more often than not it was just a box on the wall gathering dust and rust, though no doubt it would have impressed charter customers.

I recall the time I performed a pre-buy survey on a 41-foot Hatteras in Louisiana. The boat hadn't run in years and appeared to have been used as a fishing camp. I asked the Cajun who owned the boat if the old Loran A machine bolted to the bulkhead worked. Looking at me with a puzzled expression, he asked, "What's it do?"

Loran-C became very popular among offshore fishermen beginning in the 1970s.

"It tells you where you are," I replied.

"Well, I just look out the window," he said.

So, early Loran equipment was practically useless for finding an artificial reef, and everyone trolled for fish. Each day during the summer months, charter boats and recreational fishermen ventured into the Gulf in search of the nomadic schools of king and Spanish mackerel. Charter boat captains depended on their abil-

Today, GPS will put you within 3 feet of your destination.

Reef Making

ity to find the fish and fill the iceboxes to overflowing. They might spend the day chatting on the CB radio and asking their buddies on other boats if they were catching anything, knowing the answers would probably be lies or coded messages. They navigated using dead reckoning or, if they weren't good at that, at day's end they headed north until they reached the beach and then found their way to the pass.

Each captain had a loyal following of customers who depended on him or her (yes, there were female captains) to fill their freezers at home to justify the expense of the journey to Orange Beach each year.

Those were happy times, when Orange Beach was still a sleepy little fishing village where everyone knew everyone else. They fished together and perhaps some would spend their evenings unwinding at the Gulf Gate Lodge, where good food, dancing and booze abounded.

Life was good until December 20, 1984, the day the National Oceanic and Atmospheric Administration (NOAA)/National Marine Fisheries Service (NMFS) placed a daily bag limit of two king mackerel per person on fishermen in the northern Gulf. It marked the first time anyone had limited the fishing in the Gulf, and it led to widespread panic. Would the loyal charter boat patrons continue to book their treks to Orange Beach if they could not fill their freezers at home? Would vessels disappear from the marinas? Would fuel and tackle sales fall off? Would property values fall, and the home-building industry suffer? Two king mackerel per day — it was all the talk in the community and especially at the Orange Beach Charter Boat Association meetings.

CHAPTER 2

First Reef Zone

Despite the general hand-wringing, there was one captain named Armon Annan who didn't worry about NOAA's imposed limit of two king mackerel per day. Armon's boat, *Gulf Rebel*, was slow and when the king mackerel moved 25 miles offshore, the *Gulf Rebel* had a hard time getting there and back in the same day. Before anybody heard of the crisis of king mackerel limits, Armon was obtaining Corps of Engineer permits to build artificial reefs near shore. A practice that might have died with Armon in 1986, as the Corps no longer issues reef permits to individuals.

Loran-C still was largely unaffordable. To locate his artificial reefs, Armon used land ranges, as fishermen had in the 1930s. He would spot, say, a telephone pole and water tank marking one range and a chimney and a sand dune marking the other. Where they crossed, Armon built his reef. Other charter boat captains made fun of him for catching "those old trash fish," but Armon did very well and kept his fish box full of red snapper when pelagic fish were unavailable.

For his reef-building operation, Armon built a removable plywood platform that fit on the back of his boat. He collected old washing machines, dryers, refrigerators and tires. He would carry this pile of junk out into the Gulf and, using land ranges to hold the boat in position, push the reef material over the stern.

After NOAA set limits on king mackerel, local charter captains watched Armon come in each day with his cooler overflowing with red snapper. They began to see his wisdom. What sealed the deal for them was that Loran-C became affordable and they could copy Armon, except do it out of sight of land. There were a couple of reasons they wanted to build reefs offshore. Charter boat captains learned that if they didn't go out of sight of land, many of their paying customers didn't feel they'd gotten their money's worth. Secondly, the skippers knew the locations of the reefs needed to be kept secret, so they were deployed away from prying eyes.

Ignoring the requirement of obtaining a Corps permit, just about everyone began building platforms similar to Armon's and began accumulating washing machines, stoves, refrigerators, tires, toilets and anything else they could manhandle onto a boat. Everything was cabled together and hauled out to carefully selected reef sites. One popular method of deployment was tying a truck tire to one end of a 30-foot cable and the bound reef material to the other end. When a boat arrived at the chosen site, the tire was kicked off while the boat was still in gear and moving forward. When the slack in the cable was taken up, the tire dragged the reef off the stern and the boat quickly circled back over the site to record the location.

Besides the Loran-C unit, each boat needed a bottom machine (sonar) to measure the depth and show what else was down there. The early machines had a paper scroll and a wire that continuously moved on a belt against the paper. It passed an electrical current through the special paper, drawing a black-and-white picture of the bottom and painting anything protruding above the bottom — including fish. The

First Reef Zone

bottom machine was important because the Loran-C unit could only get you close, but not directly over the reef. The boat had to circle around until the reef showed up on the bottom machine. If a boat couldn't get directly over the reef, no fish could be caught. Today's sophisticated bottom machines have color TV-type screens and are so detailed they can spot a single fish. Unlike Loran, a good GPS will get you within three feet of a reef.

After a reef was deployed and located on the bottom machine, the Loran-C coordinates were recorded in a small notebook. This little notebook was the most valuable item on the boat and rarely left the captain's pocket.

To locate the reef again, the captain navigated to the Loran coordinates and circled around until the bottom machine told him he was in the right place. Each captain had to develop the skill required to hold the vessel over the reef using forward/reverse on the engine/engines while eyeing the bottom machine and the Loran-C. He had to compensate for wind and current, which isn't an easy thing to learn and is actually quite a feat. Nobody anchored, and I'll tell you why later in the story.

As more and more vessels began to build reefs, the U.S. Coast Guard started to take notice of the fleet of vessels periodically heading out of Perdido Pass loaded with junk to dump into the waters off Orange Beach. The Coast Guard had recently started enforcing the MARPOL Act, an international law created in 1980 that forbade dumping anything in the oceans, with a few minor exemptions. The MARPOL Act deemed reef material illegal without a U.S. Army Corps of Engineers permit, so the Coast Guard posted a vessel in Perdido Pass and turned around any boats loaded with reef material that lacked permits and sent them back to the dock.

Reef Making

Alarmed, the fishermen called an emergency meeting of the Orange Beach Charter Boat Association. In July 1986, they decided to ask Vernon Minton, director of the Marine Resources division of the Alabama Department of Conservation and Natural Resources (ADCNR) to obtain a reef permit from the Corps for a site in the Gulf of Mexico to deploy their reefs. Thus, armed with a permit, reef builders could sidestep the MARPOL Act and the Coast Guard couldn't stop them anymore.

Vernon Minton was a big man, not big as in overweight, but tall and massively built. He was always friendly to fishermen and did a good job keeping the peace and managing the various groups using the fishery. My relationship with him wavered between very difficult to very friendly. But no matter how different our views were, Minton would always listen to a fisherman's side and he could be convinced he was wrong and change the rules.

In fact, he would change the rules in a heartbeat if he thought it would benefit Alabama fishermen and he didn't worry about political views. Minton, who died in 2010 five days shy of his retirement date, was admired and respected by most fishermen. True to form, he took the heat when he was blamed for an unpopular rule. Minton was the perfect person with the vision to see what a truly private artificial reef program could do for Alabama. His rapport with the shrimping industry helped smooth out rough patches with agreements for sites where artificial reefs would be permitted, areas that would forever be lost to shrimpers after the Corps of Engineers issued the permits.

Next, enter John Winn of the Corps of Engineers' Regulatory Division in the Mobile District office. The Corps of Engineers oversees anything having to do with artificial reefs. Minton contacted Winn and asked for a very small permitted area (say, a square mile) for a fishing reef zone. Thank God that John Winn was in a position to make it happen! He was more than happy to help. The first question Winn asked Minton was if he could make the zone bigger. Minton said "sure," and presto: in January 1987, Alabama was granted an 800-square-mile reef zone. Today, the reef zone measures more than 1,200 square miles, making it the largest artificial reef zone in the United States. Winn, a visionary who passed away in 2016, also gave the permits to the state in perpetuity. By comparison, reef permits in Florida must be renewed every five years. That's a problem because the Corps works so slowly it takes years to navigate the renewal process. Instead, Florida has a perpetual permit renewal program, rather than a perpetual reef program.

Here's how Alabama's reef program was set up to work for private reef builders: The ADCNR got a blanket permit from the Corps for an artificial reef zone. The permit spelled out the boundaries and what types of material were permitted. Empowered by the Corps, the ADCNR could allow anyone to build reefs within the permitted area as well as add restrictions of its own.

Once it had the Corps permit, the ADCNR began to allow fishermen to use its permitted area to deploy reefs. Looking back, it represented a new and radical policy that flew in the face of normal government bureaucracy. Never again in my lifetime would the federal government act as reasonably and responsibly toward the fishing industry.

In the beginning we were given a blanket letter of permission to deploy reef material, but that changed within months of the creation of the reef program. The state began issuing reef builders a free, temporary, one-day license/permit. No reefs were built in state waters "legally." Alabama's reef zone starts 12 miles offshore and extends about 60 miles offshore. All of it is in federal waters.

Enforcement is a complicated thing. Alabama has a law that forbids transport of reef material without a permit. This law can't be enforced outside state boundaries. So, the state must catch you before you get three miles offshore. If you're caught more than three miles offshore without a permit, the state can do nothing legally, except refuse to issue that person any future permits. The Coast Guard can't enforce the state's law outside the state, but could claim the fisherman is in violation of the MARPOL Act, but only if he is seen dumping something.

There are some other peculiarities in the permitting system. For example, the MARPOL Act rules state that if a ship traveling beyond 25 miles offshore wants to dispose of something like a shipping container, it can legally throw it overboard, but if the intent is to create an artificial reef, it's a violation. Weird, huh?

The Coast Guard has jurisdiction over all vessels in state and federal waters. It can stop anyone at any time and inspect the vessel for drugs, safety equipment, proper licenses, etc. The concept of "probable cause" doesn't apply. So, when you have a bunch of 18-year-olds riding around on patrol looking for a vessel to board and I'm the only one out in December, guess what happens?

My relationship with the Coast Guard degenerated quickly to problemsome. In their minds the plastic in the automobiles I was dumping as reef material was a violation of the MARPOL Act. They didn't want to accept the fact that the Corps of Engineers could defy the MARPOL Act.

On the state level, as with any new and innovative program, rules needed to be established, but at first no one knew which rules were needed. The original permits were free and involved no time restraints, no inspections and no restrictions, and were granted in a permission letter. The system gradually changed, one rule at a time, sometimes causing temporary conflicts between Vernon Minton and me.

CHAPTER 3

Red Snapper

Much about the interaction between artificial reefs and fish was learned over time. At first, the impact of building artificial reefs and their effects on the Gulf environment were largely unknown to marine scientists and marine biologists. As artificial reefs caught on with fishermen, the scientific community tried to keep up with the rapidly expanding construction efforts. Getting a scientific handle on artificial reefs was not an easy task. Despite the millions of dollars spent in the last 30 years to study artificial reefs, only one definite conclusion was reached: "We know very little." Of course, that didn't stop people from forming unqualified opinions, and conjures up an old saying, whose author is unknown: "Beware of half-truths. You might have gotten hold of the wrong half."

The predominant species of fish associated with artificial reefs in the northern Gulf of Mexico is red snapper. In the early days of artificial reef construction (which essentially began in 1987), marine scientists disagreed about the production of red snapper on such man-made habitat. Indeed, many, if not most, marine scientists suspected that artificial reefs represented a zero-sum game and only attracted red snapper from elsewhere for fishermen to catch and kill. By 2015,

Reef Making

however, overwhelming evidence supported the concept of production, instead of attraction. Over time, most marine scientists and biologists became convinced that artificial reefs produce fish, which was something that Alabama charter boat captains learned early on.

Theirs was a logical conclusion that could be drawn from the historical records of the Star Fish & Oyster Company (circa 1860–1880s), located in Mobile. Those records show that commercial fishermen sailed their fishing vessels to a location off Pensacola previously mentioned. Red snapper only live on structure (natural or artificial reefs) and this small, hard bottom of low rocky ledges is the only inshore natural reef in the northern Gulf. Records from those times indicate that in less than five years the small fleet of sailing vessels had decimated the red snapper population in that area.

By the late 1800s, with red snapper close to home unable to support a large-scale commercial harvest, fishermen began to sail to Campeche, Mexico (over 700 nautical miles from the northern Gulf Coast), for the fish. It wasn't until oil and gas production platforms (today numbering more than 4,000) were constructed in the northern Gulf off Louisiana that red snapper began to reappear in large numbers. The tens of thousands of artificial reefs deployed over time added to the snapper boom.

Let's return to 1987 before moving on toward the present. With the newly permitted reef zone south of Alabama's beaches, charter boat skippers armed with permits began to build reefs. Within a few months, however, they realized what a chore it was. A platform had to be assembled on the stern of a boat and reef material wrestled on to it and tied together — all without scratching a paint job worth several thousand dollars. Once loaded, the captain and crew then had to wait for calm weather. Some tried to use small barges, but they had to be towed at much slower speeds and, once onsite, it was necessary to transfer someone over to the barge to facilitate unloading. One wrong move could cause the boat and barge to come together in a rough sea and it would take 10 charters to pay for the damage inflicted. Plus, if a party wanted to charter the boat while it was loaded and waiting on the weather, the captain would have to unload the material and load it again later or pass up the charter.

This is where I came in.

CHAPTER 4

First Commercial Reef Builder

In 1987, very soon after the program started, I put down my first reef about 20 miles offshore. I didn't set out to be an artificial reef builder. Indeed, I was the most unqualified person for that task. I had no degree in marine biology, no fishing experience and no offshore boating experience. In fact, I knew nothing about artificial reefs before I found myself immersed in a plan to convert a boat for that purpose. My passion was boats and their mechanics, and artificial reefs were not even on my radar screen.

My boating experience was limited to many hours as a child on Dog River in a 14-foot, outboard-powered boat that I used for skiing and exploring the river. From there it was on to the Marine Corps. After boot camp, I volunteered for a "Med Cruise," a six-month deployment on a ship in the Mediterranean. That ship, the *USS San Marcos* (LSD-25) was a fascinating piece of machinery. The voyage would include many ports and amphibious landings. I was very excited to be going there instead of Viet Nam. That came later. All went well until it got underway from Norfolk, Virginia. A queasy feeling came over me; I never threw up, but for the next six months the queasiness never left me unless I was on dry land.

Reef Making

I was disappointed that I was prone to seasickness, but my love of boats never wavered. I resigned myself to smooth-water boating in the future. After my discharge from the Marines, I found a land-based job working for the Terminal Railway at the Alabama State Docks in Mobile. During that time, I got married and settled down across Mobile Bay in Fairhope. One year into my job at the railroad, I started a part-time boat engine repair business, working out of my car on my days off. In the first year, my business didn't make more than $50 total, so I decided to use my GI Bill to go to college and become an engineer. I quit the job at the railroad but kept my part-time boat repair business. Near the end of my second year in college, my business had expanded so much that I had to choose between college and my business. I stuck it out with boat repairs and by 1985 my business had grown to the point I owned and operated a little shipyard in Fairhope. Even so, I still drove to Orange Beach and repaired fishing boats there.

Around that time, the offshore oil industry collapsed again — as it often does — and I got a deal on a 45-foot-long, steel-hulled workboat powered by twin 120-horsepower (hp) diesels. The boat cost $2,500, and I took it to my place of business in Fairhope. I picked it up with my travel lift and blocked it up in the back of my shipyard. It sat there for a year while I thought about what I could do with it. It was named the *A.W. Carroll*, but quickly developed the nickname *Reefmaker*.

One day in January 1987, Earl Griffith, owner of the charter boat *Sea Reaper* as well as a marina in Orange Beach, came to my shipyard. "David," he asked, "what are you going to do with that boat?"

"I don't know," I replied honestly.

"Why don't you convert it to haul junk cars offshore for artificial reefs?"

First Commercial Reef Builder

I had seen the washing machines, refrigerators, tires and whatnot on platforms set up on the sterns of charter boats, but cars? Earl explained that fishermen preferred scrapped cars and there was a demand for a boat to haul them out into the Gulf. As I was looking for something to do with my bargain boat, I told Earl, "If you can guarantee 20 cars, I'll convert the boat to haul them." He phoned me the next day and said he had 40 junk cars ready to go.

My first step was to enlist the help of Al West, a local welder. Getting the junkers on the boat wasn't nearly as challenging as figuring out a way to get them off the boat and into the water even in rough seas. The 45-foot boat had a 20-foot-long by 12-foot-wide cabin located at the stern of the boat. We decided to leave the cabin intact and haul the cars on the front deck, which protruded 25 feet forward of the cabin. I envisioned some type of complicated hydraulic crane,

The Reefmaker rigged out and ready to transform a boatload of junk cars into an artificial reef.

but Al thought otherwise. He said it needed to be as simple as possible, with no moving parts. We came up with a series of rails angled at 45 degrees. Each car would sit on two rails. The rails were welded to a longitudinal beam running from the top of the cabin to the front of the boat. We designed it to hold eight cars at a time. Eight chains were fastened on this beam to hold the cargo. Each car would be lifted onto the boat with a crane that I had purchased for $400 from the City of Fairhope at a public auction. The plan was to pick up the car by running a chain through the passenger and driver windows. Once the car was positioned, I would feed another chain from the boat through the frame, behind the front bumper, and then fasten together each end with a bolt and nut. The crane would then ease the car down onto the rails. I would disconnect the lifting chain and swing back to the next car waiting on land. To release the cars, I would use a cutting torch to cut the bolt and the car would slide off into the water.

Al and I completed the framework and loaded eight cars aboard at my marina in Fairhope. Four were positioned on one side and four on the other, with their front bumpers meeting at the top of the framework and their rear bumpers almost touching the water. Right from the start a problem arose. The weight of the eight cars toward the bow of the boat picked the stern of the boat out of the water and exposed the propellers. The only solution was to build two more racks on the back of the boat for a couple of additional cars, making a total of 10. This brought the vessel back to level and completed the conversion.

I made final preparations for the first voyage. I was to leave Fairhope for Earl Griffith's Marina, a trip of about 35 miles at 8 miles per hour, and from there out into the Gulf of Mexico to deploy the cars. The boat was operated from inside the cabin, though that changed

The Reefmaker's deployment system was simple, but effective.

later when I was able to procure a small wheelhouse from a salvaged Coast Guard buoy tender, which we sank as an artificial reef.

In the beginning, the noise from the engines was deafening because, except for a 3/16-inch steel deck, there was no insulation separating the engines from the cabin (perhaps due to that noise, nowadays I find it necessary to wear hearing aids). From the control station inside the cabin, the operator's ability to see where he was going was limited, except straight ahead through the triangular opening created by the eight cars hanging at 45-degree angles off port and starboard. It was necessary to frequently run to the cabin's side doors and peer out to make sure boats, markers and other objects didn't pose dangers to the vessel's navigation.

I started out of Fly Creek into Mobile Bay, running back and forth from one door to the other and then back to the steering station. All this to make sure I didn't run into any boats parked in their slips or channel markers. As soon as I cleared the sea buoy off Fly Creek and

Reef Making

into Mobile Bay, I saw only one thing that posed a potential problem: Windy Johnston in his sailboat.

It would take the rest of this book to tell you all about Windy, but suffice it to say here that he was a treasure and the most delightful person I ever met. Windy never wore socks, never was in a bad mood and never experienced anything that changed his happy-go-lucky outlook on life. For years, Windy worked at the Grand Hotel south of Fairhope as a swimming instructor. He had a working replica of an old racing sailboat that was built by Robert Jeffcott, another interesting Fairhope character in his own right. Windy loved to sail and most days would find him out doing just that.

As I made my way down the bay, I studied Windy and his boat for a moment to get an idea of their course. I could see him sitting at the tiller and underway by the one-cylinder Yanmar diesel engine. Seeing we were almost side by side on a parallel course and separated by only about an eighth of a mile, I was sure Windy saw me. If he held his course, I would overtake him with plenty of room to spare. I went back to the steering station and sat down, happy to get a break after my running back and forth.

Everything would have been fine, except Windy didn't see me and went below into the cabin, leaving the tiller unattended. It wasn't long before I heard a crash and felt the boat jerk to port. I jumped to my feet and ran to the starboard door. I saw Windy's boat dangerously close to my starboard side, dead in the water as it slid by my vessel. I went full reverse to stop the boat. I ran again to the starboard door and called to Windy, who, by this time, was on the deck of his boat and headed forward to inspect the damage.

We sat side by side for a while until we determined he wasn't taking on water and could return safely to Fly Creek. The damage wasn't bad, but because Windy was crossing my bow from my starboard side, it was my fault. I couldn't wait to drop off the *A.W. Carroll/Reefmaker* at Earl's Marina and hurry home to help Windy.

The rest of the trip was uneventful. Once safely docked at Earl's, I rushed back to Fairhope in search of Windy. He wasn't home or at his boat. A mutual acquaintance told me they had seen him at the Yacht Club Bar. I drove over and there he was, having a beer and regaling everyone who would listen with his tale. I interrupted and began to tell him how sorry I was and that he should bring his boat over to my shipyard for repairs. He laughed and told me not to worry about it. He had not seen me and went into his cabin momentarily and the next thing he knew we had collided. He said that Robert Jeffcott was coming the next day to fix it. Besides, Windy said, he was having the best time telling everyone in the bar that he was the only person in history to run into a Ford Thunderbird in the middle of Mobile Bay.

That's Windy.

CHAPTER 5

Private Reefs

The *A.W. Carroll* sat at Earl's until a good weather day presented itself. That came on an April day in 1987, three months after Alabama received its first reef zone. The boat was only equipped with a compass and a radio. To prevent me from knowing the secret location of each reef I deployed, I wasn't allowed to have a Loran. Those locations were not to be shared with anyone, not even a captain's own mother.

I should explain the difference between private and public reefs. A private reef is paid for by an individual. It represents an out-of-pocket expense. Reefs are known simply as "spots" to fishermen. Once a reef is deployed, it can't be owned by anyone. If another fisherman finds it, he or she is free to fish it. The trick is to keep the location a secret for as long as possible. Keeping a spot secret is done in a few ways. First, the exact location isn't shared with anyone. Secondly, fishermen pick locations not heavily traveled by other fishermen. In the old days, one way of accomplishing this was to deploy a reef farther offshore than anyone else. When fuel was cheap, captains leapfrogged one another to the point where we were deploying 70 miles southwest of Orange Beach. Thirdly, while a reef is fished, a constant lookout is maintained for other vessels. If an approaching boat is sighted, everybody picks up and leaves.

One trick used by non-reef owners is to take two vessels and approach the boat fishing the reef at right angles. Each of the two interlopers then heads directly toward the boat fishing at high speed. Even if the boat fishing the reef tries to move to hide the structure's location, the approaching vessels maintain their original heading. When the two vessels meet, they have found the reef's location.

Captains have a countermeasure for this. If he sees the two vessels positioning themselves, the captain will allow his boat to drift off the reef with the current a few hundred feet. Once he sees the two gatecrashers start their run, he starts to run as well. Thinking they are aiming at the reef, they actually cross or meet at a place too far from the reef to find it. Another option for the charter boat is to run directly at one boat to make its skipper alter his course. Later, as refined radar provided a method of displaying the coordinates of targets, it became even harder to hide a reef. This is the main reason no one ever anchors on his or her own spots. It would be impossible to retrieve the anchor in a timely manner before reef-stealing vessels showed up.

Mostly, fishing private reefs involved a sort of gentlemen's agreement between charter boats. Each boat deployed in a certain territory and most others respected it. The area was small enough for a captain to see if other vessels were fishing his spots. Still, some charter boats never built reefs and always "stole" the spots of others. There have been many fights and lots of angry words exchanged between fishermen. A skipper I know became so angry with another for fishing his spots that he chartered an airplane with a GPS to fly out and swoop down on the offending captain to learn the location of one of his spots. As it happened, however, the captain in the airplane discovered that his rival was anchored on one of his spots.

If a captain abused another fisherman's spot frequently enough, sometimes the offended fisherman would drop a weighted bottle of Clorox® bleach with some pinholes in it on the reef. The fish would disappear, and the spot would become useless to anyone.

Recreational fishermen represented a constant irritant to charter boats and a 360-degree lookout for "monkey boats" was the norm. "Monkey boat" was the name charter boat crews gave to recreational fishermen in small outboard-powered boats, because from a distance the men onboard the small vessel looked like monkeys running around. Charter boats were guilty of stealing spots as well. The "theft" of spots got so bad that to keep the peace some marinas began to require charter boats prove they built at least 10 spots in the preceding year.

As time went on, monkey boats began to use my services as well and joined the ranks of private reef fishermen. Pilfering reef locations still goes on today. The worst offenders are commercial fishermen who never build their own, but search and find the reefs of others. Then they anchor on the reef and devastate it with long lines or a fishing line with up to 32 hooks. They will sit there until the reef is completely fished out.

Charter boat captains developed a method for moving a car they knew or suspected of being found by another fisherman. They would send a diver down holding one end of a rope. The diver would then feed the rope through the car's window or bumper somehow and bring the end back up to the boat. The captain would then cleat one end of the rope on one side of the transom and the other end on the opposite side, and slowly tow the car several hundred feet away. Once the reef was relocated, the captain would release one end of the rope and pull it aboard. The fish on the reef would just swim along with the car to its new location. It worked then, but when we began to sink 3-ton concrete reefs the practice was no longer viable.

Hiding a reef from others can only be accomplished if the reef zone is very large and provides a lot of elbow room for fishermen to hide their spots. Other states tried to emulate Alabama's reef program, but fell short because they only allowed small zones; say, 7 by 10 miles or 3 by 15 miles. This pales in comparison to Alabama's 30-by-50-mile zone. All the reef zones off the Florida Panhandle can fit inside Alabama's reef zone with lots of room left over. A large zone is very important. A boat fishing on a spot can be seen easily from 5 miles away. So, in small zones it would be impossible to build a reef and visit it on a busy day without losing the location to another fisherman. Other states have tried to provide fishermen the opportunity to build private reefs, but few take advantage because the zones are too small. Most states require that a state official either ride on the fisherman's boat, or follow the fisherman in a state boat to the deployment site. After the reef is deployed, said official might also anchor on the reef and dive it. Plus, since state officials typically don't want to work overtime, an early morning or late afternoon deployment when other fishing boats aren't present is not a good option for the reef builder.

Alabama has a different system that is superior to others. A fisherman can deploy his or her reef without close oversight. The locations are recorded and submitted to the state after the deployment and are closely guarded. Alabama regularly uses side-scan sonar to map the entire area to confirm that the reefs are where they're supposed to be. Since side-scan is used on a moving vessel traveling in grid fashion, an interloper can't find somebody's spot simply by watching the survey vessel. Alabama's private reef program works well for everyone, but horrifies the radical environmentalists in other states, especially some members of PEER (Public Employees for Environmental Responsibility). For some reason never adequately explained, these PEER members believe private reefs are a terrible idea. They continue to fight hard to make sure private reef building is discouraged and the process is too restrictive for any fisherman to consider it. However, they haven't been able to influence Alabama officials.

A "radical environmentalist" is someone that takes a position against something and refuses to discuss ways to solve the problem. For example, they might take the position, "No oil refineries," but fail to recognize everyone needs gas to power their cars. Wouldn't it benefit everyone if we tried to solve the problems associated with having a refinery close to home, instead of refusing to discuss it?

When it comes to artificial reefs, I think the radical environmentalists are missing an important point. Private reef builders learned early on that if a boat catches all the legal-sized fish off a reef in one day, that spot will not produce another legal fish for a year. On the other hand, if the reef is managed properly, by fishing it sporadically, it will produce fish year-round. Putting it another way, our concrete pyramid might be good for 500 pounds of red snapper per year if fished conservatively, but only about 50 pounds per year if hammered on a regular basis. This conservation practice is one example of the few times capitalism and environmentalism have worked together. Management produces more fish, replenishes the fish stocks and follows good environmental practice. The reason why continues to go unexplained by marine scientists and biologists. Charter boat captains discovered this method and still practice it religiously to this

Reef Making

day. It doesn't mean public reefs don't produce fish as well, but they do so at a reduced rate.

In a nutshell, here's what happens on a typical trip: A charter boat carries its party to a reef, then they lower baited lines. The captain looks over his shoulder at the quantity and size of the fish being landed. Once he judges that the reef has produced enough fish without overtaxing it, he allows the boat to drift off the reef. The party surmises that they have exhausted the reef's fish because they aren't getting any more bites. The captain announces it's time to pull up and go to another reef. Mission accomplished. The party is catching fish and the captain is conserving fish on his reefs. His livelihood depends on it. And all the efforts by radical environmentalists to curtail private reef building are actually impeding the recovery of fish stocks, instead of helping it.

CHAPTER 6

Public Reefs

Tax dollars finance public reefs, and the location of reefs are published for everyone to fish. Florida has a yearly grant program funded by revenue from fishing licenses and federal tax money. Alabama builds public reefs whenever federal funds in the form of grants are available to it. Mississippi does the same thing. Louisiana rarely builds artificial reefs and the permit process is nearly impossible, as it might take years to get one artificial reef approved. This is puzzling because Louisiana has the richest reef fund in the world. It's so big that the state's legislature kept raiding the fund to pay for other projects, to the tune of more than $46 million.

In 2014 Louisiana voters overwhelmingly approved the Louisiana Artificial Reef Development Fund Protection, Amendment 8, to keep lawmakers from snatching cash out of it. Currently Louisiana only has a few dozen public reefs, compared to Alabama's 40,000-plus. Texas has a very active artificial reef program and builds hundreds of reefs inside its nine-mile boundary. States along the Atlantic Coast build artificial reefs as well, but nothing like the states bordering the Gulf of Mexico.

Reef Making

The National Marine Fishery Service (NMFS) imposed seasons and limits on red snapper, which in effect suppressed the production of red snapper on public reefs. For the most part, public reefs are raped on opening day, wherever and whenever that might be. All the fishermen leave the dock on opening day and hit the public reefs. Even private reef owners do it. Boats sit on the reefs until there are virtually no more legal fish to catch. Only then do the private reef builders move to their own reefs. The public reefs struggle to produce a few more legal-size fish, and then the cycle is repeated the following year. I repeat, even a public reef continues to contribute to an increase of the biomass of red snapper and other species. It's just that it would do much better if it were managed.

I attend reef conferences on a regular basis. I listen to a lot of scientists and marine biologists who present results of studies. What is evident in every one of the presentations is the realization that they know very little about the workings of artificial reefs. Study after study provides contradicting data. Despite all the money handed out for studies of the breeding, spawning, migration, feeding habits, habitat needs, etc., of most species, much is still largely unknown.

I recall an international reef conference I attended in Biloxi, Mississippi. Toward the end, 17 of the world's leading experts on artificial reefs were invited to sit on the stage and field questions. I stood up and asked the question "Why, if a private reef is fished out in one day, won't it produce another legal-size fish for another year?"

There was silence and the experts began looking at each other as if they were hoping someone would jump in with an answer. Finally, one asked, "What's a private reef?" Surprisingly, none of the world's leading experts on artificial reefs has ever heard of a private reef or the private management of a reef. I realized at that moment that the charter boat captains of Orange Beach knew more about artificial reefs than all the world's leading experts. Unfortunately, the rest of the world largely ignores this incredible wealth of knowledge, even though millions of dollars are spent in research.

CHAPTER 7

Trust

In my first days of reef building, I was merely a conveyor. The charter boats supplied the cars, obtained the permits and selected the locations. On my first trip offshore, the plan was for me to follow a charter boat out into the Gulf of Mexico to the chosen reef deployment site. At some point the captain would call me on the radio (Marine VHF radios have a 1-watt switch that limits the range of the radio) and tell me to stop and deploy the reef. I would stop, cut the bolt holding the chain together and the car would slide off into the water. I would move away, and the charter boat would wait for the car to sink and settle before recording the location. Then I would follow the charter boat about a mile away and drop another car. Distance matters; charter boats still like to place their reefs about a mile apart. It saves time and fuel when fishing. One mile seems to be the magic number to prevent another fisherman from happening onto a second reef.

Once I deployed the last car, the charter boat would set a course for Perdido Pass and I would follow in its wake. Loran-C, like the GPS of today, had a feature that allowed coordinates for Perdido Pass to be entered and provided a compass bearing to the sea buoy. Following in

Reef Making

the captain's wake, I would take note of the compass heading and steer that course until I arrived at the pass as well. It sounded like a good plan, but it didn't work out very well. I could only go seven knots; the charter boat could go 20 knots. Soon the charter boat would be out of sight while I was still steering its course, which theoretically should still put me at the sea buoy as well. Now, imagine a one-and-a-half-knot current running to the east and we are both headed due north. Let's say we are 30 miles offshore when we both decide to head home. He will be there in an hour and a half. It will take me more than four hours. We are both drifting with the current east at a rate of one and a half knots while heading north. His Loran-C can calculate his speed and eastward drift during his hour-and-a-half run, while compensating to provide an accurate compass heading. If not, he would be two-and-three-quarters nautical miles east of the pass.

I bet you can see where I'm going with this. During my four-hour trip, I'm going to drift six miles to the east. I have no idea there is a current and since I don't have a Loran, I have no way of knowing how to compensate for it. I won't reach the pass, but rather a beach more than three miles east or west of the pass, depending on current direction. If it's nighttime, and it usually was in those days, all I can see is a beach and maybe some homes. I have no way of knowing where the pass is, east or west.

During subsequent trips, I continued this arrangement, which left me complaining about the navigation problems. Finally, the fishermen began to trust me enough so that I could equip what had now become generally known as the *Reefmaker* with a Loran, but not turn it on until I was a couple of miles away from my last drop.

Within weeks of my completion of the *Reefmaker*, Earl invited me to move to his marina — complete with my crane. A deal was struck that stipulated I would haul all of Earl's cars for free in exchange for dockage. By this time, I had sold my shipyard and was operating a bar and restaurant on another vessel I owned. I was still plagued with seasickness, especially at night or when I had to go into the engine room. So, I hired someone to run the *Reefmaker* and concentrated on other projects.

I lived on a houseboat at Walter Trent's marina, which was next door to Earl's place. The deal was that I didn't have to pay rent, and got water and power in exchange for 10 car reefs per year. About a year into this my *Reefmaker* captain got a better offer and wanted to move on. I leased out my bar and restaurant and took over the reef business again. I began to run the *Reefmaker* vessel and the more I ventured offshore, the more immune to seasickness I got. It was still early in the artificial reef program and I was learning new things daily, such as how to prepare reefs, what to charge, what to pay for a car, how best to load the reefs, how to read the weather, how to deploy without being seen, which locations worked best, how far apart to deploy cars and that sort of thing. At the same time fishermen were developing techniques for managing the reefs as well as where to deploy them, how long to wait to fish them, determining which reefs worked best and why, which types of reef produced which species of fish, and so on. Relying on my actual experience and listening to the reports of hundreds of fishermen, I developed a great knowledge of artificial reefs to share with my customers.

Finally, fishermen who didn't trust me before with a working Loran began to trust me to deploy the reefs without oversight. Also, I began to purchase cars and sell them to the fishermen. I would receive a list of coordinates for the 10 cars. Some would specify which make and model to drop at each spot. Some guys still didn't trust me entirely

Reef Making

and wanted to go along. That was fine with me; they would run the boat while I cut the cars loose. I began to obtain permits myself. I would call the ADCNR on the phone and they would send somebody to the *Reefmaker* to inspect the cars. All fluids had to be drained and the car steam-cleaned. Once the inspection was complete, I was issued a permit. The permit listed the reef zone I intended to deploy in, (Alabama has five zones, but all are connected, except for narrow shipping lanes running through them), a departure time and a return time, and which pass I planned to use. We had a choice of two passes, Perdido/Alabama Point and Mobile Bay. A permit obtained today was good tomorrow or sometime in the future, but not to exceed 30 days, and only for one day of deployment. Weather was the biggest factor in choosing days to deploy; we tried to pick days of seas that were three feet or less.

In the beginning some boats tried to follow us, hoping to wait for a car to drop and obtain its location. This was usually not a charter boat, but a recreational fisherman in a monkey boat or else a commercial fishing boat. Once I dropped a car it floated, sometimes for as long as about 20 minutes. I was amazed to learn that Buicks floated the longest. It didn't matter which year or model.

The floating cars presented a problem at night, before deploying at night was outlawed. If the car drifted out of sight, it was almost impossible to find it again before it sank. I discovered that most cars were manufactured with a hole in the floorboard on either side, each plugged with a big rubber stopper. I could knock out the plugs and the car would sink much faster.

I developed our own system for dealing with any offending reef-stealing pursuers. I would turn the *Reefmaker* sideways to the pursuing vessel so those aboard couldn't see the far side of our boat.

Then I would take a bucket of leaves and perhaps other biodegradable debris and dump it over the opposite side from the interloper. Then I would pull away at full speed. I would watch the boat speed ahead and begin circling the debris using his bottom machine to try and find the reef. I would be miles away before the captain realized he couldn't find anything. If I had already deployed the car and failed to notice a boat charging toward us, I would turn the *Reefmaker* and head directly at it, forcing the captain to turn to avoid us. This would interfere with his navigation toward the spot and delay him long enough to have any debris drift away with the current and wind. After that, he could never find the reef.

Usually there wasn't much interchange between reef builders and reef bandits. That wasn't always the case, however. I recall when a charter boat captain named Sandy Smith, a former professional baseball player who has since passed away, got into a bit of difficulty. He was fishing his spot when he noticed a small vessel approaching at high speed. Thinking the vessel was a reef stealer, he headed directly toward it to force its skipper to change course. At the last minute he discovered it was a U. S. Customs boat. Captain Smith was arrested for attempted assault of a federal officer.

The beauty of using cars for reefs is that they rusted out in about five years. By that time, another fisherman or two might have found them, but still they had served up around 500 pounds of red snapper each year for an original investment of about $250. Cars had lots of complex spaces for little marine critters to hide from predators and steel makes for good reef substrate. Cars were cheap and easy to deploy. I don't recall any report of debris or pollution from cars floating onto beaches, but now I shudder to think of what some might

Reef Making

say about using such an unseemly environmental no-no. Today, the notion of using cars as reefs is farthest from anyone's minds.

The *Reefmaker* did not have a bottom machine, and even if it did, I never developed the skill of finding a reef using a bottom machine. My job was to pilot the boat to a location provided by the fisherman and dump the car overboard. At first, I believed the cars might sail or glide underwater to locations away from the *Reefmaker* boat. To test that theory, I used a rod and reel with old fishing line obtained from the tackle store. The deckhand would tie the fishing line to the car and once it hit the bottom, I would move the *Reefmaker* around until the car was directly under the boat. At that point I would record the location and break the line. Eventually I discovered that cars didn't sail and wound up directly below where they sank or else within 50 feet, good enough for fishermen to find. The rod and reel was retired.

Rarely would a fisherman attempt to find a newly deployed car. One auto by itself is very difficult to find with a bottom machine and only the most experienced fishermen equipped with a very good bottom machine can find a single car. Knowing that, fishermen wouldn't look for the car, but instead the cloud of fish above it. It took about a year for the reef to develop a good population of fish. Some charter boat captains waited up to three years before attempting to find and fish a car.

Some reefs never produced fish. Even those of us with years of experience in such matters still don't know why. Some reefs produced so many fish that when the boat pulled up to the spot, the water around the boat turned red with snapper. Unsuspecting vessels trolling for king mackerel often discovered red snapper on their lines when they trolled across one of these "hot" spots. But it's not always snapper that swarm over reefs.

Frank Bros, a local charter boat captain, once took a group of divers out to one of Alabama's Liberty Ship reefs. On the way back to the dock, Frank ran over a reef that "blew up" on the bottom machine. That means a large cloud of fish was displayed on the screen. The divers asked if they could dive it. Frank circled back and they suited up and went down. Not more than two minutes later they came back to the surface screaming they wanted to board at once. The spot was loaded with hundreds of triggerfish. Triggerfish have sharp teeth for eating barnacles and coral, so when the divers began to descend, they were attacked by the hungry fish. All their wet suits had holes and some of the bites penetrated far enough to remove pieces of flesh.

Fish have their preferences. I found that reefs made with tires seemed to produce more triggerfish while cars, vans, buses and other metallic reefs produced mostly red snapper. Later, I learned that manufactured reefs with large interior spaces produced gag grouper and goliath grouper — especially the farther east you went. Conversely, the farther west you went, the more snapper one encountered.

CHAPTER 8

Economy and Rules

In 1987 Orange Beach, a little-known rural community with only a few fishing boats, began to explode into the number-one fishing destination in the Gulf of Mexico. The expansion of the reef system was a prime mover. Red snapper recreationally caught in the Gulf off Orange Beach went from almost zero in 1987 to being 42 percent of the total recreational catch by 1993. Not bad, considering Alabama only has 1.5 percent (45 miles) of the coastline. All of this was due to the thousands of private reefs deployed. No tax money was used, and all the cost was borne by fishermen. Reefs were environmentally managed and red snapper stocks exploded — all without governmental help or intervention.

Until 1990, Destin, Florida, was the capital of fishing on the northern Gulf, but over the years fair claim to that title slipped away. A fisherman told me a story about fishing in Destin that sums it up nicely. He and his buddies regularly chartered fishing boats in Orange Beach, but one year they decided to try a change of venue and went to Destin and chartered a boat there. The fishing was just as good as it was in Alabama. The ride was longer, but they caught a lot of red snapper. It made them wonder why everyone was bragging about fishing in

Alabama, because their results were just as good out of Destin. Later, at the dock, they talked to the captain and asked about the general proximity of his fishing spots. He told the men that he had run to Alabama waters to fish.

In the early days (late 1980s), fishermen in Destin could build private reefs as well. The City of Destin had a reef zone and gave fishermen private permits to sink cars, as was the case in Alabama. I could obtain a Destin permit by facsimile machine and I deployed a lot of cars over there. That changed when the Florida's Department of Environmental Protection (DEP) took over and restricted private reefs. Later, Florida Fish & Wildlife took over the state's control of artificial reefs and added more restrictions. Things changed again when the state returned the reef zones to county oversight, but it tacked on restrictions for private reefs. After that, a true private reef program never emerged in the Sunshine State.

There is a misconception about the economic history of Orange Beach. Most people think the community was built on tourism dollars boosted by condo sales. Orange Beach owes everything it is to fishing. The economy in the 1990s did not flourish because a snowbird financed a condo so he could lie on the beach all day. It grew because hundreds of people came to fish, rent hotel rooms and eat in restaurants. Owners of half-million-dollar fishing boats arranged dockage at marinas, hired captains and crews, spent money at local tackle stores and purchased fuel. While this guy was fishing, his wife and kids were spreading more money around town. Gulf Shores rode on Orange Beach's economic coattails to become what it is today. There might be an argument now about the cash generated by fishing versus sunbathing, but in the 1980s and 1990s there was no contest.

Economy and Rules

As fishing in Alabama exploded, marinas in Orange Beach were being built as fast as land, permits and material could come together. Land values exploded, houses and condos seemed to be going up everywhere. New charter boats arrived every day. The fleet went from less than a dozen to more than 120. There were economic bumps along the way, but each downturn gave way to a new boom. The reef program strained at its hinges, with new official rules from the state and lots of unwritten rules for fishermen.

The growing fleet of charter boats ventured out each day through the pass en route to their private fishing spots. Every charter boat kept its bottom machine running as soon as it left the pass until it returned, always on the lookout for a reef to pop up on the screen. If it did run over a "new" reef that it hadn't deployed, the skipper would record the location. If the boat fished it at all, chances are its occupants would respect the reef owner and only catch a few fish. That was an acceptable practice and most charter boats adhered to the code. Occasionally, but not often, a charter boat would anchor on someone else's reef overnight. This was the worse type of offense. Not only is the skipper planning on catching all the fish, he is serving as a marker beacon for any other boat –recreational or charter — to pull up and make note of the location. Only the least respectable fishermen did this.

Six years into the reef program (1993), problems with shrimpers arose. Meetings between the shrimpers and the ADCNR hammered out areas for the reef zones that were not normally places where they shrimped. Everything went well until artificial reefs began finding their way into shrimp nets. Shrimpers complained that some fishermen were not putting their reefs in the zones, but it was common knowledge that if shrimpers found shrimp in the zones, they put on old, tired gear and went trawling. If they lost their gear, they didn't lose much. Some shrimped in the zones, dragged reefs outside the boundaries and then complained about them anyway.

Later that year, in September 1993, a new law required that a sticker be placed on each permitted reef that identified the owner. Each reef permitted had a number that could be traced back to the owner. The ADCNR tracked down the owners of reefs found outside the zone and began to prosecute them. The reef owners claimed they had stayed in the reef zone and either shrimpers dragged the material outside the zone with their nets or the current moved it.

The conflict heated up, with shrimpers wanting to limit reef deployment only to commercial reef builders, or to shut down the program completely. There were only two full-time commercial reef builders at that time. Vernon Mitton didn't want to take away the right of every fisherman to build his own personal reef. To placate the shrimpers, he began to outlaw any reef material found in the shrimpers' nets, which fishermen claimed had moved via current outside the zone. Banned were semi-trucks, fiberglass boats, shopping carts, washing machines and anything that incorporated metal thin enough to become detached from the reef and be carried away by current. Over the next couple of years, the list of acceptable material grew smaller and smaller. Even so, the new rules solved the problems and complaints ceased.

Almost none of the banned material was likely to shift, but when an accused reef builder claimed it moved somehow, it was added to the forbidden list. In truth, reefs have been known to move during hurricanes. Charter boats have reported cars relocating up to 400 yards along the bottom. Through trial and error, charter boats would search for and find their reefs after each hurricane. Once they got over their wayward reef, they could calculate the direction and distance

Economy and Rules

from the original spot. Believe it or not, other savvy captains were able to find most of the lost cars by searching the same distance and heading from the original spot. The fish would just swim along with a reef to its new location. The newer concrete modules we manufactured didn't move at all during hurricanes.

Chicken transport devices aka "chicken coops" are the cages used on trucks to transport live chickens over the road. We used to call them chicken coops, but radical environmentalists were horrified and complained that wooden chicken houses as seen in farmers' backyards were not suitable reef material. So, we had to rename them. They are 8 feet long 4 feet wide and 5 or 6 feet tall with shelves. They make great reefs, but disappear during tropical storms or hurricanes. At first, we thought they must have moved, but later found they bury into the sand, sometimes uncovering later. We discovered that attaching one to the side of one of our concrete pyramids prevents it from burying and makes an outstanding reef.

In 1999 a $50,000 bond was required to transport reefs after daylight hours. Later, it was changed to daylight hours only, period. I was told the nighttime rule came about because of an incident in Florida when two fishermen decided to sink an old boat for a reef. They prepared the vessel and began to tow it offshore. Both fishermen were on the towboat. It was dark, and the towed vessel began to sink. They continued on, unaware of the problem. It would not have been that big of a problem, had they obeyed the one cardinal rule I have for towing: Never use a towline shorter than the depth of water you are towing over, that way if the boat sinks, it will hit the bottom without pulling the tow boat under as well. When the towed vessel abruptly sank, it pulled the tow vessel under, drowning both fishermen.

Reef Making

The daylight-hours-only rule caused me more problems. The reef zone was so large that if I left the dock at daylight, by the time I made it to the outer limits of the reef zone it would be dark. It was against the law to transport or deploy reefs at night. So, it was a catch-22 situation.

More rules had to be made. In the end, reasonable rules solved all the problems.

By 1993, the ADCNR's standard operating procedure was to place a sticker on the reef material identifying it as permitted reef material. In 2005, a law was passed that carried a $25 fee for each reef. Now the permit fee is $31.

CHAPTER 9

Coast Guard

There came a time I found myself struggling to get enough cars for customers, adapting to changing rules and fighting with the U.S. Coast Guard. Dealing with the Coast Guard was the worst of my trials. The Coast Guard, which was a branch of the Department of Transportation and is now part of the Department of Homeland Security, has what I consider to be an adversarial relationship with the U.S. Army Corps of Engineers, the real keeper of the keys in the reef-building world.

Incidentally, after Alabama received its artificial reef permitted area in 1987, the Coast Guard didn't bother me until around 1990. They shut down a reef-building vessel in Destin, the *Reef Runner*, for threat of pollution. For some reason, the owner of this vessel, whom I had never met, named me as his partner. That triggered the ADCNR to refuse me permits. It took a while, but I pushed back at the Coast Guard and eventually was exonerated. I think the *Reef Runner* piqued the Coast Guard's interest in reef builders, and I don't think they believed that I wasn't part owner in the *Reef Runner*.

To set the stage, first consider the MARPOL Act, the international law enacted by all nations with access to the sea. In 1984, the Coast

Reef Making

Guard had just completed training for the enforcement of the new law, which, among other things, states that no plastic over 1-inch-square may be dumped into the ocean. Cars have lots of plastic, but the Corps says that the plastic is okay if it's a car permitted by them for an artificial reef. The conflict that ensued over this interpretation was the source of much pain and aggravation for me.

I was caught in the middle of these opposing powers and the Coast Guard showed no mercy. During the 1980s drug smuggling was rampant along the Gulf Coast. The Drug Enforcement Agency (DEA) had radars on tops of condominiums in Orange Beach and the Coast Guard always had a patrol boat out in the Gulf. In the winter, fishing effort was virtually nil, so guess who had the only vessel venturing out into the Gulf from Orange Beach? It became almost routine: The patrol boat skipper would either see me on his radar or the DEA guys would spot me on their radar and alert the Coast Guard patrol boat. Either way, the *Reefmaker* and I became something for them to do on patrol. Each time they stopped me, they would always ask over the radio: "What is the nature of your voyage?" I always thought this was a funny thing to ask. Here was a boat loaded with 10 junk cars onboard. Did they think I was a ferry that got lost?

Next, they would demand that I stop. I stopped. Then came the boarding, a demand to see the reef permit, a search for drugs and, when none were found, there nevertheless was always some little something wrong with the safety equipment to justify the boarding. It wasn't just me. For instance, there was Brian Annan, Armon's nephew who took over Armon's business after Armon died. Brian runs a meticulously maintained charter boat. Once, the Coast Guard stopped him and the inspecting officer couldn't find so much as a single tiny violation. Perplexed at having stopped the first vessel he ever encountered that didn't have some minor violation, he called his superior on the radio and asked for advice on how to proceed.

On the *Reefmaker*, I was not as diligent as Brian and always got a citation for something or other. One time it was because my bell wasn't the correct size. The rules state you may substitute a frying pan and spoon or a gong for the bell. I kid you not. On this occasion, the Coast Guard officer told me, "Your bell is too small for this size vessel." No problem; I had a pair of oxygen/acetylene cylinders strapped to the wall that I used in burning the bolts to release the cars. I picked up a big hammer and walked over to the large oxygen cylinder. I looked at him and asked, "How about this?" I hit the cylinder as hard as I could. Someone unfamiliar with a burning rig might think that this was suicidal, but I knew better. It's harmless. The Coast Guard officer almost dove for cover, thinking an explosion might follow the hammer blow. And there was the ear-shattering sound the hammer made against the steel cylinder. He winced at each blow while I was trying very hard not to laugh. I kept hitting it with a straight face until he demanded I stop. Nevertheless, I still got a citation for the bell because he couldn't find anything else.

It was always something with them: There was the time the reflective tape on my life preservers (PFDs) wasn't bright enough, and the time the gauge of one of my fire extinguishers was just barely out of the green zone. Whatever offense was involved, the result was always the same: we were ordered back to the dock and issued a boarding report. The boarding report was a sort of citation accompanied by a fine. My first boarding report stated I owed $20,000 for a life preserver reflective tape violation. Luckily, I found out that there was an appeal process. If one said he was poor, which I was, it could be negotiated down to as little as $50.

Reef Making

One time the Coast Guard stopped us when we had two semi-trailers chained on. The semi-trailers protruded high above the *Reefmaker*, but also a couple of feet below the water. The drag they created reduced our speed to two knots. The patrol boat stopped us late in the afternoon about 25 miles offshore. I can't remember what they claimed the violation was, but as they began to escort us back to the dock, one of them called on the radio and said, "You guys can speed up, we can keep up with you." I replied, "This is as fast as it will go." Twelve and a half hours later, at 4 a.m., both vessels arrived at the dock. The Coast Guard was only equipped for a short-day patrol. Those aboard had no water or food for the 12-hour ride following us to our dock and had too much pride to ask us for some. I couldn't help but chuckle to myself as the blue uniforms made a mad dash for one of the garden hoses at Earl's Marina to quench their thirst.

As I got better at appealing citations, I discovered it was possible to get the fine dismissed altogether if you could find anything remotely wrong with the boarding report. I remember being stopped about 30 miles offshore. It was a slick-calm day. As the Coast Guard boat circled around the *Reefmaker*, the crew noticed a Ford station wagon on the back. Those particular cars hung almost vertically. A couple of drops of gasoline dripped from the gas cap of the station wagon and we've all seen the sheen on the water that causes. The tank was drained, but unbeknownst to me a few drops must have remained somewhere in the system. The motion of the vessel dislodged it and it ran down into the filler pipe. Gasoline is almost never a pollution cleanup emergency. I'm not advocating that it's okay to dump gasoline in the water, but a few drops will evaporate off the water and harm nothing. But the Coast Guard can issue a citation; I suspect it's their favorite one.

They wrote me up that day. I composed an appeal, and just for the fun of it I noted that, "This is not my problem. If gas was dripping from a Ford gas cap, it must be a defective gas cap and Ford Motor Company should be cited instead of me." Unbelievably, it worked, and the charge was dropped. I don't know if they ever cited Ford.

It's interesting to note the 41-foot Coast Guard vessels of that day were equipped with model 903 Cummins diesel engines. At idle, the entire area behind those vessels had a diesel fuel slick coming out of the exhaust pipes. It's the nature of that engine. So, there they were, writing me a citation for fuel sheen that was 10 times smaller than the one coming out of the stern of their boat.

The constant harassment came to head in 1996. The Coast Guard knew me by name and seemed to have it out for me. In November of that year, the Coast Guard stopped my vessel late one afternoon. The *Reefmaker* was two miles from the deployment site and more than 10 miles offshore. I had all the proper permits and the pastor of my church was running the boat. He loved the sea and, on his days off, ran the *Reefmaker*. I was happy for the break in the grueling 20-hour days of those busy times.

By the way, as noted, Alabama had rules for deploying reefs and one of those rules stipulated that reef material couldn't be transported after daylight hours. These rules were converted into law and were attached to a $5,000 fine. All things considered, this is an interesting law. The reef zone starts 12 miles offshore and the State of Alabama's territorial boundary ends at 3 miles offshore. So, Alabama laws can't be enforced past 3 miles. However, even though a violation might not be legally enforceable, it could result in them refusing me more permits. I could lose either way.

Reef Making

Back to the Coast Guard stop of November 1996. When the Coast Guard calls you on the radio for a boarding, you must slow to an idle and wait for the crewmen to come alongside and board. It was very rough that day and a fiberglass 41-foot Coast Guard boat coming alongside a rusty steel hull is always an interesting experience. In a rough sea, even the most skilled captain might leave some fiberglass on the steel hull. I guess the crew was debating this, but they found a solution. After sitting there and stalling for about 30 minutes, they didn't bother to board, and just told my pastor over the radio that, "It is official sundown; you are in violation of the Alabama law concerning transporting reef material after sundown. Turn around; we are escorting you back to the dock."

My pastor complied and when he was within cellphone range, he called me and told me what had happened. Both vessels arrived at Earl's Marina about 8 p.m. and I was there waiting. Once docked, the Coast Guard guys searched and inspected the *Reefmaker*, and found a couple of safety things. One of those they noted while still offshore was that they couldn't see my stern light because of the cars hanging off the back, which wouldn't have been there after dark if the pastor could have deployed them, which he couldn't because the Coast Guard had stopped him.

I was livid about the whole episode. The phone call from my pastor gave me some time, before they arrived, to check the rules. I looked up the daylight rule and found it referred to "daylight hours," not "sundown." I kept a copy of Black's Law Dictionary in my houseboat, so I looked up "Daylight Hours." It is defined as, "when a person's face is discernible," while "Sundown" is defined as "the moment the Sun dips below the horizon." That's a difference of about 30 minutes or more. Add that to the 30 minutes the *Reefmaker* was held up and there was plenty of time to get to the deployment site and deploy the reefs without violating the nighttime rule.

So, I was ready for the Coast Guard officer when he arrived at the dock and I don't recall being kind or humble. As he tried to hand me the boarding report, I informed him of the daylight-sundown deal and the fact that he was trying to enforce an Alabama law outside the State of Alabama. I told him in no uncertain terms that it amounted to false arrest and I would be pursuing legal action against him. Since he had not boarded the vessel offshore, he did not have another excuse for ordering us back to the dock. I was bluffing and hoped it would make him reconsider.

It brought up another point of law. Alabama laws only apply to humans. If the Alabama Marine Police charges somebody with violation of a marine law, the citation is issued in the name of the person operating the vessel. However, if the vessel is a Coast Guard-documented vessel, the Coast Guard issues boarding reports in the vessel's name. Thus, documented vessels are an entity that can accumulate debt, be arrested and sued, etc., just like a human. In effect, the Coast Guard officer was using an Alabama law intended for a human and applying it to an inanimate object (my boat). I figured it would be interesting to see what a judge would make of this.

For a while we shouted at each other, or maybe I was the one doing the shouting. Anyway, at around 9 that Friday night, the Coast Guard officer handed me a boarding report and left. The ADCNR had already been contacted and told that I was responsible for making reefs after dark. Nothing could be resolved until the following Monday, when administrative personnel for the Coast Guard and the ADCNR arrived at their offices. Over the weekend, I corrected all the safety violations noted in the boarding report and Monday morning the little *Reefmaker* legally left the dock and deployed the reefs. I stayed home and called the ADCNR authorities and told them my side of the story. Then I waited for someone to blink.

At 11 a.m. the Coast Guard boarding officer called and said he wanted to meet with me at noon. By that time the *Reefmaker* had returned. At our meeting, he handed me a second boarding report almost identical to the first, including the date and time. He asked me to return the original report. I refused. He said it didn't matter; the second one replaced the first one. The second boarding report terminated the use of the *Reefmaker* due to a hole in the floor of the cabin. It stated the vessel was unseaworthy. After reading it, I was shocked. He left, and I pondered my next move.

What he had done with the stroke of a pen had put me out of business. I guessed it was a feeble attempt to cover up his mistake of turning me around for no legal reason. The ADCNR would not issue me another permit, due to the Coast Guard's action, and the Coast Guard would arrest me if I tried to operate the boat. Repairing the boat was out of the question. The entire floor would need to be replaced. The vessel was seaworthy, but beyond her serviceable life. The entire reef program was changing, and in one month, the little *Reefmaker* would be obsolete, but I needed her until December 31 to deploy the last of the cars. After that date, no more cars would be allowed. As of December 31, 1996, Alabama outlawed the use of cars as reef material and restricted the material list to almost no materials of opportunity.

As noted, the *Reefmaker's* official and original name was the *A.W. Carroll*, a boat from Otis Wireline Service. She was designed for inland water operation to service oil platforms in the marshes of Louisiana. Surprisingly, she handled heavy seas very well, behaving like half boat and half submarine. She would hit a large wave and almost stop. The wave would come crashing over the bow and flood the deck two feet deep. This required me to install a watertight door in the front of the cabin. The water rushed back, sloshing up the front of the cabin and running off both sides. At the same time, the boat would regain forward motion until the next big wave. The hundreds of reef trips in rough water, which she really hadn't been designed for, had taken their toll. The bow was a square bow like a tugboat. Over time the entire bow began to curl up like an old shoe wrinkling the steel deck. Rust covered up most of the cabin; no paint had touched the topsides in years. The entire cabin floor was rusted with lots of small holes, but only one big one as noted by the Coast Guard.

Armed with two boarding reports for the same incident, I started making phone calls. It took me about a week, but I finally was able to talk to a Coast Guard official who was appalled that I had two boarding reports issued the same date and time, and stating two different things.

Then stuff began to happen. I got a call from the boarding officer. He wanted to make an appointment to reinspect my vessel. He arrived, and his demeanor was curt. Without discussion, he went about his business of inspecting the now-corrected deficiencies noted in the first boarding report. Finally, he handed me a document stating all the items on the original boarding report had been corrected and I was free to use the vessel. He went on to say that he was being forced to resign his commission because of me. I felt no sympathy.

At this point, one might think that all unpleasantness was behind me. With my Coast Guard-approved, seaworthy vessel loaded with 10 cars, I applied for and received a reef permit. The next morning my captain set off westward for a deployment near Dauphin Island, over on the southwest side of Mobile Bay. The wind was out of the north,

Reef Making

so my captain hugged the beach for a smoother ride, until he got due north of his deployment area about 12 miles offshore. He headed south with the waves for a smooth ride, deployed the reefs in accordance with the permit and bucked a sea back to shore to return home the same way he came.

I reloaded the next day and applied for a permit. The ADCNR wouldn't issue one. I was informed the Coast Guard called and told the agency I was not to receive another permit. The Coast Guard charged that I was caught in Florida making illegal reefs. The ADCNR told me the Coast Guard instructed them not to issue me any more permits. I called the Coast Guard and nobody there wanted to talk to me. It required a lot of calls and pestering for a couple of days, but finally, I got a Coast Guard officer to blurt out, "We caught you in Florida making illegal reefs. We have aerial photos. The photos and report are on the way the federal prosecutor's office. You are going to federal prison." Talk about a shock to the system, I couldn't believe what I was hearing. Being in Florida meant I was not in Alabama's Reef Zone and therefore without any legal right to deploy reefs or it would be a violation of the MARPOL Act and Alabama rules. I called my captain and reconfirmed his route and the reef locations in the opposite direction from Florida. What was going on? How could they have pictures of my vessel in Florida when it had gone in the opposite direction? Was the Coast Guard framing me for a crime I didn't commit?

The captain and I jumped in my truck and headed to the federal prosecutor's office in Mobile to plead our side of the case, hoping to head off any indictments. On the way, I had a thought. I called the ADCNR and asked if my competitor was making reefs on the same day. My competitor was Steve Rhodes. He purchased a boat several years after I started in the reef business and rigged it the same as mine.

Except he could carry five cars on each side and none in the back. I even let him come over and measure my boat, to configure his. We were friendly competitors and there was more than enough business for the both of us. The contact at the ADCNR said Steve was making reefs the same day as I was. I called the Coast Guard back and asked if the pictures contained the name of the vessel. His reply was "Yeah, as if there are two boats like yours hauling junk cars." I replied, "There are. The name of his vessel is the *Peggy Lynn* and mine is the *A.W. Carroll*." I never officially named the boat *Reefmaker*; it was just a nickname.

There was a long silence on the other end of the phone. Then he finally said, "I'll call you right back." He didn't call, but the ADCNR did. The person on the other end of the line told me the Coast Guard had called and said it was alright to issue me a permit. Before reaching Mobile I turned my truck around and went back to Orange Beach, where I received a permit for our next trip.

The Coast Guard had a vendetta against me. The day I supposedly went to Florida waters, they sent out two Falcon jets with cameras. They burned thousands of dollars of fuel combing the Gulf and eventually followed a vessel they thought was mine for hours, taking pictures. Since the *A.W. Carroll* was hugging the beach headed west, they didn't notice her just outside the sandbar next to the Alabama coastline. They were looking farther offshore. The only other boat was Steve's. The two jets tag-teamed, one relieving the other, refueling and returning to take hundreds of pictures of what they thought was me illegally making reefs in Florida.

Once they confirmed that the name *Peggy Lynn* was on the boat, they realized they had brought charges and a lot of grief against an innocent man and possibly put him out of business. Believe it or not, they never phoned Steve Rhodes or me, and I think they just wanted this mess to die a quiet death. I wasn't going to let that happen.

There is a government form, "Form SF-95," that is a simple claim form against the government. I filled it out and mailed it. I stated that the Coast Guard owed me $25,000 for illegally putting me out of business for two weeks. It triggered a formal internal investigation by the Coast Guard. Using the Freedom of Information Act, I requested a copy of the investigation. With the investigation report as my evidence, the claim went before a Coast Guard judge. Of course, he ruled against me. But after I lost in the Coast Guard court, I could appeal to the federal circuit court. I let that hang over their heads until a week before the statute of limitations lapsed. I requested a meeting with the Coast Guard. I went by myself and sat on one side of a large conference table. The Coast Guard had a team of attorneys on the other side. I offered to drop my appeal on two conditions. I wanted a letter of apology and a promise that the Coast Guard would leave enforcement of Alabama reef rules to the Alabama authorities. I got the letter of apology and, since I was never bothered again, I assume the Coast Guard honored the second part. I heard it had escalated into a big deal at the Coast Guard base, with lots of reprimands passed around. It must have left a lasting impression, too. About a year later, I called the Coast Guard to ask an unrelated question. The person I wanted to talk to was not there. When I left my name and number with his secretary to call me back, she asked, "Is this, 'the' David Walter?"

CHAPTER 10

Car Dealer

During the 10 years between 1987 and 1997 when cars were legal reef material, I deployed over 10,000 automobiles. Business was so good that at one point I fell 18 months behind in reef orders. Because I was buying every available junk car within 50 miles, I might have been the South's largest used car dealer. I offered more for junk cars than the junkyards and purchased as many as I could. I had some good guys as regular suppliers, but a lot of people that search out junk cars and sell them to junkyards are not the finest citizens. They are a strange lot: unkempt and weird, and some very scary. Standard business practices didn't work; they required cash — no checks and no IDs. I dealt with folks who had names like "Wing Nut," "Ace," "Buck," and "Gator." I had to carry a couple of thousand dollars in my wallet to be prepared for a delivery of cars at any time. Earl didn't like the mound of junk cars piling up at his marina and I couldn't blame him. He found a piece of property for me to purchase. It was across the street from Earl's Marina, behind Jones' Canvas, way back off the road next to a swamp. It was the ideal place to store the cars out of sight.

Reef Making

I bought a forklift and truck and trailer to handle the growing pile of cars at the end of the solitary dirt lane leading to my newly acquired lot. I would select cars from the growing stacks and pile them on the truck and trailer. I would transport them across the street to the boat, load them with the crane and repeat the process until the boat was full.

I don't know why I'm not dead. For some reason, the strange group of car sellers that supplied me never came around during daylight. They would knock on my houseboat door at all hours of the night and I would have to drive across the street and down the lane into dark stacks of cars, armed with a flashlight to make sure they actually delivered a car. Yes, a couple of times they tried to claim they delivered a car, when they did not. I paid different prices according to the size and condition; mostly "condition" meant it wasn't half a car. I negotiated the price depending on condition: burned-out cars, halves of cars, and cars missing doors, truck lids, hoods and tops had different prices than complete cars. Large cars received a premium price. Whenever I made a purchase, I would dig into my bulging wallet and pay cash for the car. No receipt, no title, no bill of sale.

These cars were not drivable. Most had no engines, transmissions or any other valuable items remaining. I did get some stolen cars. There was the time one of my best suppliers stopped showing up. All his cars arrived in nice shape, and not rusty or missing doors, fenders and the like. I found out he was in jail. There was a good reason his cars were so nice. He would cruise the interstate and if he saw a car parked on the side, he would chain it to his pickup, take it somewhere and strip it. Next, he would load what was left of the car on a trailer and deliver it to me, effectively destroying the evidence. He finally got caught stealing generators from oil rigs in Mount Vernon, Alabama, and was sent to prison. He seemed like such a nice guy that I never suspected his cars were stolen.

My small junkyard served other purposes. The local hot-rodders used it as a source of parts. I allowed this practice if they limited their pilfering to small parts. However, the pile of cars served its best purpose for birthday parties for my two young sons. Birthday partygoers would be given old baseball bats and be turned loose in the junkyard. Windshields, headlights, taillights, hoods and fenders were all battered until everyone was exhausted. Kids always said our parties were the best.

At first everyone just wanted cars. Then they wanted only big cars. Then they wanted only station wagons. Next it was vans and then school buses. Before it was all over, the preferred reef material included cotton pickers, combines, grain silos, semi-trucks, Cobra helicopters, F4 aircraft tail sections, other types of airplanes, fire trucks, cement mixer drums, fuel tanks, shipping containers, fiberglass boats, boat molds, dump truck beds, beer trucks, Coca-Cola© trucks, concrete pipes, voting machines, ATM structures, playground equipment, conveyors, commercial air conditioners, chicken transport cages, cranes, crane booms, shopping carts, homemade reefs and other stuff I can't describe or remember. Some material was so big I thought it might turn the little *Reefmaker* over. Whatever arrived, if it was permittable, I prepared it and loaded it onboard.

Cement mixer drums were my least favorite material to haul. They didn't fit the rails very well and in rough weather they would roll around crashing into things. Even on my new boat, the *Maranatha* (more about that vessel later) they were difficult to secure. One fell off just outside the pass in about 15 feet of water. I had to alert the Coast Guard and mark it with a buoy. It sat there for about a month

Reef Making

before I was able to get permission to remove it and line up all the gear and help I needed to do so. I hired Brian Annan, nephew of Armon Annan, to dive down and tie a line to it. He attached the line to our crane hook and I lifted the drum onboard. Legally, this was a tricky procedure. The ADCNR had no protocol for this unusual operation. After some discussion and assurances that I would be taking it back to my dock and not redeploying the same day, permission was given.

All went well. Using the *Maranatha's* 20-ton crane, we lifted the drum onto the back deck and secured it. We came back through the pass and through the channel leading to the Intracoastal Waterway (ICW). Next, we were rounding Bear Point in the waterway.

I had recently hired a young man and this was his first trip on the boat. He was an avid fisherman and spent all his days and nights off work, fishing from the pier or the beach. He talked, ate and dreamed fishing. I was in the wheelhouse, piloting the *Maranatha* around Bear Point. Suddenly he burst into the wheelhouse and said, "I think we have a problem." I asked him what the problem was. He said that the Alabama Marine Police were coming up behind us with their blue lights on. I scoffed and said, "That's not a problem, because I have permission." He said, "Well, the cement mixer drum is full of juvenile red snapper (under the legal size) and I've been filleting them on the back deck." I was dumbstruck. I just sat there staring at him. Next, he asked, "What do you want me to do?" The fine for illegal fish was $500 per fish. He had already filleted about 20 and the drum contained at least a hundred more.

By this time the police boat was coming alongside. The *Maranatha's* deck was about 8 feet above the water, so when the officers came alongside, they were below the deck and couldn't see his fish-cleaning operation. I decided to 'fess up, take my lumps and fire my new hand. I came to an idle, pulled the engines into neutral, walked out on the wing deck of the bridge and peered down at them. They looked up at me and said, "Sorry, we just talked to the office and you're okay. We thought you might be doing some type of illegal activity." I smiled and waved as they pulled away and I never had to open my mouth. We disposed of what illegal fish were left by throwing them overboard after the Marine Police boat was out of sight.

CHAPTER 11

Ships

Alabama's reef program was originally designed for small private fishing reefs. Captains realized that large reefs, such as barges and big boats, made very good reefs, but were easily found by other fishermen. The greater expense for a large reef was recognized as a much greater loss after other boats found it. Consequently, charter captains rarely made big reefs.

Large reefs such as derelict ships typically were not deployed as fishing reefs, but as reefs catering to scuba divers. Larger reefs were popular in Florida where scuba diving was considered as being on the same level with fishing. This was not the case in Alabama; scuba divers were generally considered to be a nuisance during the heyday of red snapper from 1987 through 2000. Charter boats and divers didn't get along back then. That has changed dramatically over time and nowadays divers are a welcome addition to Alabama's marine recreation industry.

During that time, Escambia County, Florida's Artificial Reef Committee was actively looking for large reefs to be deployed on their reef sites. One day I got a call from Eileen Beard, who with her partner, Gene Ferguson, owned a dive shop in Pensacola named "The Scuba

Shack." Eileen told me that Escambia County had a $25,000 grant to sink a vessel. They had contracted with someone to sink a steel-hulled vessel, but the deadline was approaching, and the guy couldn't be located. The grant would expire soon, I was told, and they would lose the money if a vessel could not be procured in short order.

Besides being out of touch, this person had a questionable reputation. He deployed one other vessel off Pensacola, but the locals were skeptical about his capability. The vessel he sank was a small steel-hulled boat. On the day of deployment, I was told, he hired a boat to tow the vessel offshore. When he arrived early that morning, he jumped onto the reef boat, slipped and broke his leg.

Instead of scrubbing the mission and heading to the hospital, he hobbled onto the county's observation vessel and insisted the crew carry on. He said he needed the money badly. He then collapsed onto a bunk, obviously in great pain. All efforts by the crew of the observation boat to compel him to go to the hospital were rebuffed. Reluctantly, they proceeded out of Big Lagoon through Pensacola Bay Pass and into the Gulf to the deployment site. When they reached the spot, he was unable to move from the bunk and get onto the vessel to start the sinking process. He asked the county's observer if he could sink the boat for him.

The observer was an elderly man, but stated he would do what he could. To everyone's surprise and horror, the young man leaned over the side of the bunk and opened a bag he had brought along. He pulled out a fully automatic and loaded AK-47 rifle. He told the observer to get aboard the vessel, lean through a window and shoot holes through the bottom of the vessel to sink it.

Fortunately, the observer knew guns enough to perform the task, but he was concerned about ricocheting bullets. The young man suggested he just stick his arm through a window and pull the trigger, telling the observer the steel cabin and deck would protect him from errant bullets. Skeptical, but assured by the injured man that it would work, the observer transferred from the observation vessel onto the boat without much difficulty. Then, standing on the side of the cabin and putting the hand holding the rifle through the window, he pulled the trigger. The selector switch was on full auto and the AK-47 blasted away. Suddenly the observer felt a great pain in his right arm and quickly retracted it. A bullet had ricocheted and hit his wristwatch, destroying it. But, by the Grace of God, other than giving him a small bruise, it had done him no serious harm. This episode, which included many hours of waiting for water entering through the bullet holes to sink the vessel, greatly reduced the number of observer volunteers who wanted to accompany this same person on another deployment.

So, Eileen asked if I could find an old boat to sink for the Pensacola reef team. The payoff, $25,000, seemed like a fortune to me, and all I had to do was acquire a boat and sink it. In Buras, Louisiana, near the mouth of the Mississippi River, I located an old 60-foot tugboat

Sylvia

Reef Making

named "Sylvia" rusting away next to the levee there. I found the owner living nearby. He agreed to a purchase price of $5,000. I bought the tug, went back home and set out in the *Reefmaker* to Buras. I took the tug back to Orange Beach. I cleaned it up, towed it to where the Pensacola folks wanted it and then sank it. It was the easiest money I ever made.

Soon, the Pensacola folks had another $25,000 to make a reef. I found another tugboat named the "Heron" in the Mobile River for $2,000. It had been sunk at the bank of the river for a few years, but was easily raised during low tide and didn't need as much cleaning. The years it had been submerged underwater completely washed any fuel, oil and grease away long ago, so almost no cleaning was required. I did notice that the bow compartment contained some junk and a large roll of manila rope, but there was no hazardous material that required removal. The coil of rope was huge, but too rotten to salvage and it would be difficult to remove. Since manila rope is organic, I left it to be sunk with the tug. I gave it a once-over to remove some salvageable items and it was ready to go.

Then came a bonus. The Pensacola reef committee found an LCM sunk at the Gulf Islands National Seashore dock in Mississippi. LCMs are 56-foot-long landing craft seen in war movies depositing troops on a beach. They wanted to know how much I would charge to get it up and sink it with the tugboat? We agreed on a price and I took the little Reefmaker over to Mississippi. I pumped the water out of the LCM and towed it back. It didn't need much cleaning either, since it had been sunk for a long time as well.

My sinking plan was simple: I would tie the two boats side by side, open a valve in the tugboat and, while it was slowly sinking, I would use a torch to cut a hole next to the water line on the LCM. The

Ships

The LCM, *the tug* Heron *and the little* Reefmaker.

sinking tug would pull the LCM down low enough to allow water to pour in the hole I cut. After cutting the hole, I would step off and let them both sink together. After all, the first boat had been so easy, this should go easy as well.

The day came to sink the boats. By then I had learned it's never good weather when you sink a boat, no matter what the forecast is. I tied the two boats together side by side, rigged a towline to the *Reefmaker* and we got underway. Within the first hour the wind began to pick up. As it got rougher, I learned something else. Boats that have holes in them, sitting on the bottom for any length of time get sealed up with mud, leaves and other debris. They appear to be seaworthy and hardly leak at all. However, when it gets rough, the water starts to slosh around inside the hull. It washes out the mud plugs and the boat or barge begins to sink. Although I didn't know this beforehand, it shouldn't have been a big deal anyway. I had a trio of 3-inch pumps, more than enough to handle any leakage problems — or so I thought.

My captain, Jerry Alexander, and his best friend Frank Bros manned the *Reefmaker* and I had Jerry's unreliable brother-in-law on

Reef Making

the tug with me. As the boat rocked and rolled, the water in the bow compartment began to slosh back and forth. I noticed the water in the bow compartment began to rise as the holes in the hull opened up. As the bow got lower in the water, waves began to break over. This was not good, I decided, and I regretted that I had cut a hole in the deck of the forward compartment for easy access. As the bow sank lower in the water due to the leaks, waves coming over the bow could run down thru the opening. Between the leaks and the waves, it could start to flood the compartment and things could get out of hand quickly. When the forward compartment got enough water in it, the tug would nose-dive, allowing water to enter the doorways and sink it along with the LCM.

I grabbed a 3-inch pump. Each pump had a 10-foot-long suction hose with a strainer on the end to keep debris out of the pump. In went the suction hose to the bow compartment. The pump was started and primed. Soon gushing water came out of the discharge end of the pump and I felt confident we had saved the boat. But no sooner had the water started to pour out than it stopped. I thought something — perhaps a rag — had covered the strainer stopping the water flow. We pulled the suction hose out of the bow compartment and found the trouble. A thick cake of rotted manila rope coated the outside of the strainer. The water sloshing around had mixed the rotting rope into a slurry in the bow compartment. We took a second pump. I unscrewed the strainer to prevent the rope from clogging it, hoping the pump could digest the rope slurry and spit it out of the discharge side. We inserted the suction hose into the bow compartment, started the pump and within a minute water was streaming out onto the deck and overboard. All was going well, and the water in the bow compartment began to recede. I relaxed. Within two minutes, however, the discharge flow from the pump began to diminish and was soon reduced to a trickle. It didn't take long to realize the pump itself was clogged with more manila rope. I didn't have the tools or the time to disassemble the pump and clean it. So, the third pump with a strainer was brought over and the suction hose was inserted in the bow compartment. The pump motor wouldn't start.

By then I was down to the original pump with the cake of manila rope on the strainer, the oldest and worst looking of the lot. The water was rising, and waves were beginning to crash over the bow. Our direction of travel into the wind and sea made the situation worse. I called Jerry on the handheld radio and told him to head downwind back to Orange Beach to keep the waves behind us. If we could make it back to Orange Beach, we would repair the holes, regroup and find another day to deploy. We were three hours into the trip and it was about three hours to enter safe harbor in Orange Beach.

I went back to the only working pump, scraped off the cake of manila rope from the strainer with my fingernails and reinserted it in the bow compartment. I started the pump and the same thing happened. I pulled the suction hose out of the compartment, cleaned off the strainer, inserted the hose and repeated the process. I left Jerry's brother-in-law to continue this operation over and over while I contacted Jerry on the radio. We still had about three hours to go to reach Orange Beach. Heading downwind bought us time because there was no danger of sinking from waves breaking over the bow. However, the rate at which the water was rising, despite our furious attempt to keep the pumping going, would sink the tug before we reached safe harbor. If it was going to sink anyway, it would be better to sink in deeper water where the wreck would not be a hazard to navigation. Otherwise, there was the expense of having to salvage it and move it

Reef Making

to a safe location. If a wreck has at least 55 feet of water over its highest point, the Coast Guard won't make you move it.

I needed Jerry to turn back south, but then I had an idea. Maybe we could tow the boats backward to keep the waves from breaking over their bows. That way we might make it to deeper water. I called Jerry on the radio and told him what to do. Jerry stopped and the brother-in-law and I moved the towline to the stern. Jerry tightened up the slack, but we quickly found that it didn't work. The two vessels — lashed together and towed by their flat sterns beating against the waves — were uncontrollable. We couldn't make any headway.

Jerry called us on the radio and confirmed that towing backwards wasn't cutting it. The boats were zigzagging from one side to the other and we were sitting still. We decided to go back to towing by the bow and head for deeper water as quickly as we could. Meanwhile, Jerry's brother-in-law and I were pulling the suction hose up, scraping off the rope with our fingernails, reinserting, restarting the pump and repeating the process. We were losing the battle. I noticed the brother-in-law had donned his life preserver and he had a strange look on his face. He sat down and said, "I quit. Get me off this boat. I can't swim. This tug is going to sink and I'm not going to be on it when it does."

He refused to do any more work. I called Jerry and informed him of his relative's proclamation. Frank Bros was not a hired hand, but a friend of Jerry's and mine. He volunteered to help. Jerry came alongside and the two guys swapped places. The towline was moved to the original location on the bow and we got underway again.

Frank and I were fighting the pump and not winning the battle. The water continued to rise in the bow compartment, but if we kept up the furious pace of cleaning the strainer, we slowed it down. We developed a routine for scraping off the rope and repriming the pump.

Ships

It was exhausting work and hard on the fingernails. The suction hose was made of very stiff material, plus it was full of water, adding to the weight and making each cycle a backbreaking exercise. So far, the LCM was not causing any trouble and required no attention, except that the two vessels had worked some slack in the lines between them and were slamming together in the rough seas. Frank decided to take up some slack in the lines. Somehow, he managed to get his thumb under one of the lines as the two boats were moving independently up and down. The line went tight and cut off the end of his thumb.

I removed my shirt to make a bandage. I called Jerry on the radio and he knew just what to do. He sent out an emergency radio call, not to the Coast Guard, but to the charter boat fleet on the frequency the captains use to communicate with each other. Within 15 minutes a charter boat arrived, transferred Frank aboard and headed back to Orange Beach. More radio calls had someone waiting at the Pass to transport Frank to the hospital. If we had called the Coast Guard, even with a helicopter, it would have taken a couple of hours just for the copter to arrive. Using a friendly charter boat, Frank was in the hospital in just over an hour. As it turned out, it was just the end of his thumb and no bone was damaged. A couple of months in bandages and the end of his thumb grew back.

Meanwhile, on the tug, I kept up the struggle. It was a bright sunny day and the sun beat down on my shirtless body as I pulled the hose in and out, restarted the pump and repeated the process over and over. Gradually, the amount of rope began to decrease and each time the pump ran a few seconds more before clogging up. At least by then we were in water deep enough to avoid a salvage operation and Jerry came back on course to the deployment site. After a couple of hours of steadily fighting the pump, I managed to get it to run for a full five

Reef Making

minutes each go-around. The water began to recede. I took one break to rig a blue tarp over the bow to give me some shade. I tied one side of the tarp to the railings on the cabin and the other to the push knees and got under it. With no shirt, my entire upper body was burned from the sun and my lips were cracked and bleeding. The shade was wonderful, and I returned to the tiresome job of pulling the suction hose out, scraping off the matted rope, reinserting the hose, restarting the pump and repriming it.

After another hour I was able to pump the compartment down to a safe level. I called Jerry and asked how much longer we had to go and he said it would be three more hours. That information was not welcome. I didn't have enough gas onboard to keep the pump going continuously for another three hours. I only had about an hour-and-a-half's worth of fuel left. There wasn't any gas on the towboat either — all of the hard work only to lose everything for lack of gas.

I had cleaned so much debris out with the pump that the water in the bow was becoming clearer. I looked down through the opening in the deck and saw strange green-neon lights in the bottom of the boat. It took me a minute to realize that they weren't lights at all, but holes. I was looking through the bottom into the clear, beautiful water of the Gulf of Mexico. I peered down into the compartment and noticed floating driftwood, left over from the time the tug was partially submerged in the Mobile River. I had a sudden brainstorm and quickly dropped down into the compartment carrying the large hammer I had on board. The water was cold, but felt good to my sunburned body. It was chest-deep and rapidly rising.

It wasn't a comforting feeling to be there. It could get ugly fast if a rogue wave broke over the bow or the water rose much higher and the bow dipped below the waves. The inrushing water through the deck opening would prevent my escape and I would go down with the tug. I tried to work as quickly as I could. I picked the biggest hole, about 2 inches in diameter. I chose a piece of driftwood whose diameter was about the size of the hole. I took the hammer and a deep breath, and plunged underneath the water. The driftwood was too small. I surfaced and chose a bigger piece. I took another deep breath and this time the wood fit much better. It wasn't perfect, but it slowed down the incoming water considerably. I then had to come back out and pump some more.

I went in again and plugged three more smaller holes, then came out and resumed pumping. By that time the compartment had pumped down nearly to the bottom, or enough that the pump began to suck air. I shut the pump down and was able to wait 20 minutes before having to pump again. The 20 minutes felt like a reprieve from heaven, but meanwhile I was so thirsty my mouth felt like it was packed with cotton. Brother-in-law had consumed all the drinking water hours earlier. I would have given just about anything for some water, but there wasn't any on the towboat either. Maybe brother-in-law drank it all. At least the gas supply would be enough to get us on site, and that gave me some comfort.

After what seemed like days instead of hours, we arrived at the deployment site. Gene and Eileen of the Scuba Shack were there on their vessel, the *Wet Dream*, and Gene had marked the spot with a buoy. Jerry slowed down, brother-in-law took in the towline until we were about 10 feet apart. It was rough, and I didn't have an anchor, so we had to use the *Reefmaker* to position the boat onsite. Jerry used the engines to hold the buoy directly in front of the *Reefmaker*. The tug and LCM sat 10 feet behind as I prepared to move tools, pumps and other equipment onto the *Reefmaker*.

Reef Making

Brother-in-law got on top of the cabin of the *Reefmaker* and threw me a line. One by one, I tied the line to the pumps, hoses, gas cans and tools. He then pulled them up and let them swing over onto the *Reefmaker*.

I had one more thing to do. My plan was to open a sea chest valve in the engine room of the tug so it would sink. It takes a long time to sink a vessel that way, but at least it gave me time to cut a hole in the side of the LCM lying next to the tug.

We reversed the sequence and brother-in-law attached a cutting torch to the line and I pulled it over to me. The oxygen and acetylene bottles remained on the *Reefmaker* and we had more than a hundred feet of hose to allow me to use the torch on the LCM.

I climbed into the LCM and began to burn a hole in its side. The procedure for burning metal goes like this: You adjust the mixture of oxygen and acetylene to obtain a bright blue flame. You hold the flame next to the metal you want to burn. When the metal is heated to a cherry-red glow, you squeeze a trigger and a pure jet of oxygen shoots out the middle of the flame to cut through the metal. At this point the torch can be moved in any direction, leaving a cut a fraction of an inch wide. If you pull the trigger of pure oxygen too soon, before the metal gets cherry red, nothing will happen. Try as I might to heat the metal, the waves lapping up on the sides between the LCM and the tug prevented the metal from getting hot enough for it to work.

I had already opened the valve and the tug's engine room was flooding. Plus, the bow compartment was filling from its leaks as well. The LCM was high and dry, and I had no other method to sink her.

Then I remembered that an LCM has a bow ramp that opens when it arrives at the beach loaded with troops or vehicles. The ramp is held closed with latches and cables hooked to a winch, so the ramp can be lowered and raised. I used the torch to cut the cables holding the ramp closed. The ramp came crashing down into the water. The hinged part of the ramp wasn't below the waterline, but the far end of the ramp hung down a couple of feet below the surface. The LCM should sink once the tug pulled it down enough for the water to enter the ramp area. At least that's what I hoped. I walked back to the bow of the tug with the torch in hand and noted the rising water in the bow compartment. Then I noticed that lying there next to my foot was another 3-inch suction hose that I failed to see before. I called to brother-in-law to throw me a line for the hose. He tossed one over and I tied it onto the suction hose. My plan was for him to pull the hose over, then the torch, then have Jerry ease back for me to jump aboard.

I glanced back at brother-in-law to tell him to pull the hose over. He had abandoned the line tied to the hose and moved to the tow bit located on the lower deck at the stern of the *Reefmaker*. He was frantically untying the towline between the *Reefmaker* and tug/LCM. I yelled, "Wait; I have to get off first." The expression on his face was enough to make me turn and look at the LCM as it was slipping underwater. He was trying to save his own skin, surmising, correctly, that if the boats sank still attached to the *Reefmaker* they would pull it down with them. The ramp hanging down from the LCM acted as a scoop picking up an occasional big wave and depositing it into the cargo area of the LCM. The LCM was going down, but the tug was still floating. I was still holding the suction hose in my hands as I felt the tug jerk sideways and begin to turn over.

By this time, the brother-in-law had untied the towline from the sinking vessels and was staring at me with an "I'm-sorry-you-are-going-to-die" expression on his face. Not yet: still holding the suction hose attached to the line on the *Reefmaker*, I jumped off the bow into

Reef Making

the water. At the same time, I realized I didn't have enough strength to swim. I yelled, "PULL!" At least brother-in-law was able to do that. I was worried about the suction from the vessels sinking pulling me down with them. He picked up the small line attached to the suction hose and hauled me the 10 feet over to the *Reefmaker*, where I let go of the hose as he pulled it onboard.

The torch hoses were the only links between the *Reefmaker* and the sinking vessels. I was holding onto the side of the *Reefmaker*. It was only two feet to the deck, but I didn't have the strength to pull myself up. Brother-in-law was no help as he froze while watching the vessels sink 10 feet away. I turned to look at the sinking boats. The LCM went first and pulled the tug over on its side. Because they were still tied together, both boats then went down. As they slipped beneath the water, air escaping from the vessels spewed up foamy geysers on the surface. I thought, "Well at least we got them sunk in the right place, but Jerry is going to have to help brother-in-law haul me aboard."

Torch hoses temporarily connected the Reefmaker *with a pair of vessels destined to become new fishing reefs.*

Ships

No sooner had that thought entered my mind then the tug lurched back out of the water not more than five feet away from me. Like a whale breaching. Then it rolled upside down and slipped underwater for the last time. The lines holding the tug and the LCM together must have broken. The tug had still contained enough air to float and come back to the surface. I've heard of people motivated to perform superhuman feats, but never experienced it until then. Suddenly my body sprang from the water like a rocket onto the deck of the *Reefmaker* and I rolled next to the cabin into the fetal position. Brother-in-law looked like a trapped rat with no place to run. Next to me was the hose to the torch bottles. It began to pay out, first slowly, and then at a furious rate. I realized that the torch was still on the tug, but I was too tired to care. The hose would break and I would have to buy another torch or, if I was lucky, some diver might retrieve it. Suddenly, the hose stopped paying out and it went slack. Brother-in-law picked up the hose and without much effort pulled the torch back from a hundred feet beneath the Gulf, undamaged.

I made it inside the cabin and collapsed onto a makeshift bed near the back of the boat. I asked Jerry again if he had any water. He said no. I asked him to call Gene on the *Wet Dream* and ask for water. Those guys didn't have any either, but did have a frozen liter bottle they used for ice in the fish box. I said, "I'll take it." They came alongside and tossed it over to brother-in-law. It was still frozen solid. Lying there, I removed the cap, placed my mouth on the bottle and with both arms cradled it between my naked breasts like I was a baby. The bottle was cold, but it was more important to melt the ice. I cradled and sucked until I had melted and sucked the bottle dry. I fell into a deep sleep and didn't wake up until I heard the engines come to idle as we passed under the Perdido Pass Bridge.

Reef Making

The LCM wound up on its bottom and the tug landed upside down with the wheelhouse in the LCM's cargo area, leaving the bow of the tug protruding upward at a 45-degree angle. Gene and Eileen loved the way it landed and said it made a much better dive reef than had the sinking gone as planned. I was happy for them, but never again did I leave the dock without a comprehensive sinking plan, a backup plan and a backup plan for the backup plan.

CHAPTER 12

More Ships

I enjoyed deploying large ships and to date have done a couple of dozen. I got better at it over time, but in the early days of artificial reef building it involved a serious learning curve. Florida continued to look for ships to sink. Eileen Beard deserves most of the credit for that. Her tireless efforts to obtain grants from the Florida Fish and Wildlife Conservation Commission made her the queen of shipwrecks off Pensacola. She even had a reef named after her. Eileen and I developed a great working relationship. I would find a large vessel and she, somehow, always managed to squeeze the funds out of the state to pay for it in the form of a grant.

By that time, my network of sources was getting better. People were calling me about old vessels they wanted to get rid of. One was an old clamshell dredge named the *Avocet* that was owned by Ratcliff Materials in Mobile. It had done its job in Mobile Bay for many years. Radcliff Materials sold out to another company and it moved the dredge to Louisiana until clamshell dredging was finally outlawed. The dredge was for sale, and cheap. I presented it to the Escambia County Reef Committee, and they raised the money. I bought it and had Brown Marine tow it to their shipyard in Orange Beach where I

Reef Making

began to prepare it. It was a big job and I struggled to get 50 years of gunk out of the bilge, as well as remove mattresses and doors. There were other items that had to go as well. The biggest problem was the stern. It was filled with enough foam to float 1,200 tons. Imagine sinking the 250-foot-long vessel in 100 feet of water with the stern still protruding above the water.

When foam floatation was introduced as a cure-all for leaking barges, everyone thought it was a great idea. The foam is pumped into a barge in liquid form. It expands to form a solid block. Later, it was learned that the foam traps water between the foam and steel plating, causing more rust and wasting the metal away faster than if foam had not been used at all. Once the barge had rusted away around it, the expense of disposing of the foam was astronomical. Also, the foam gradually soaks up water, reducing the carrying capacity of the barge over the years. Since the foam is flammable, usually no shipyard could or would attempt to repair the hull.

I had an idea. Maybe I could get the Navy to blow off the stern with C4. That would sink the dredge and I would have the stern section towed back to Brown Marine shipyard. I knew a man who wanted the stern for a barge. I needed to have both the Navy and the sale of the foam-filled stern firmly in place before I agreed to purchase the dredge. I contacted the Navy demo team in Pensacola. They seemed excited about the challenge and wholeheartedly agreed to do it (As of this writing, they still love to sink vessels and will do it for free). However, over the years I learned, using explosives sometimes severely damages the vessel and is impossible to accurately control the sinking. Also, it is harmful to nearby sea life. I developed another method of controlled sinking without using any explosives. It allows a stabilized flooding, guaranteeing the vessel lands on its bottom, upright and completely intact.

My friend agreed to purchase the stern section for a dollar, and I agreed to tow it to his place after we deployed the dredge. At that point, I purchased the dredge. Unfortunately for my scheme, I didn't get any of this in writing.

The dredge was towed from New Orleans to Brown Marine in Orange Beach, where I arranged dockage for cleaning it. I got busy working on removing the oily gunk in the bilge. It was quite a problem. I would remove all the floating oil and the next day there would be a new layer. One day I was busy at this task when two Naval officers came aboard. I had already begun cutting a 5-foot-wide opening across the entire vessel where the separation of the foam-filled stern section was to take place. Next, I was going to remove the framing to expose the sides and bottom for the C4 explosives to be attached. I assumed the Navy was there to plan the sinking, but that wasn't the reason for the visit. The two officers informed me they would not be blowing up the dredge because they were concerned the stern wouldn't completely separate and would leave the vessel in a precarious condition. I asked, "Why don't you use twice as much C4?" They replied, "It's too expensive." I said, "I'll pay for it." They said, "Our boss said to tell you 'No.'"

Suddenly the problem with the oily waste paled in comparison to this new development. I was caught in a no-win situation. I owned the dredge and because of the foam it was unsellable even as scrap. I had a contract with Escambia County, Florida that I couldn't get out of. Stopping altogether would mean certain bankruptcy, but going ahead risked the chance of catastrophe.

Reef Making

No longer having a plan for removing the stern, I thought that perhaps I could remove the foam. How does one remove foam from a boat? I was told it was highly flammable and one had to be careful using a cutting torch around it. So, that might be a possible solution. I removed a hatch exposing the top of the foam and tried to light it. It wouldn't burn. I thought it might be an oxygen problem. I purchased a leaf blower and poured some diesel fuel on the foam, turned on the leaf blower and, using a torch, got it burning. I watched it closely. Breathing in the fumes isn't good for one's health, so I kept upwind during this process. After an hour the deck turned cherry red around the hatch. After two hours of burning, I turned off the leaf blower and the fire went out. So much for being highly flammable. I measured the amount of foam burned. It was imperceptible. I calculated it would take months to burn out the foam. Even if that worked, once the foam burned to the waterline, water would enter the severely leaky hull and put the fire out. Even if I could remove all the foam, the back end of the dredge might be so badly deteriorated I couldn't patch all the leaks and it would sink at the dock. No shipyard would touch a foam-filled barge and even if they would, the cost would greatly exceed any profit I stood to make.

I phoned a friend who worked on the Mobile riverfront for the same company that sold me the dredge. He told me the company had a lot of large broken concrete blocks it wanted to get rid of. I rented a barge and, using the *Reefmaker* as a tug, loaded the blocks and transported them back to Orange Beach. I called my dock-builder friend Ray Waller and asked if he would bring his crane and barge to lift the blocks onto the dredge.

I had no way of calculating the weight needed to sink the foam-filled compartment. Sure, I was told the amount of foam could float

1,200 tons, but it was badly waterlogged. So, the floating capacity of the waterlogged foam would either be light enough to allow the dredge to sink or good enough to cause the entire dredge to float like a fishing cork. I only had about 150 tons of concrete blocks. I started praying and hoping for two things: the 150 tons of concrete ballast would be enough, and/or the foam was waterlogged enough to sink with the dredge. I also hoped that if I could sink the dredge stern-first, the weight of that front part of the dredge might force the stern to the bottom. And maybe the water pressure at the target depth of 115 feet below the surface would collapse the foam enough to reduce whatever buoyancy was left and keep the dredge sunk. By the way, this type of foam does not pose an environmental problem. Worms and triggerfish would consume all the foam in six months, passing it harmlessly through their digestive tracts.

The big day came, and Brown's tugs showed up to take the dredge under tow. I followed with the little *Reefmaker*. By that time, I figured I had considered all scenarios and what to do if this or that happened. The big tug towing the dredge had a fire monitor (firefighting nozzle mounted on the top of the cabin). Once anchored, the tug would lay alongside and shoot water into an opening I created for the Navy's demolition team. The hole was located just ahead of the foam-filled end. I had created an extensive sinking plan and designed it so the dredge would sink stern first and then flood forward to sink evenly and land upright.

The towing went well and several hours later the dredge was anchored on site. About three dozen boats came to see the sinking. I had two plans in mind. The first one specified that if the dredge sank successfully, I would collect the biggest check of my life and take a few days off to fly to the Bahamas. The second plan stipulated that if the

Reef Making

dredge sank with the stern protruding above the water, I would still fly to the Bahamas, never to return. After the tug anchored the dredge, it came alongside and began to pump water into the opening. The foam-filled stern began to sink below the surface. I was feeling better. The tug's captain, Gary Bryant, a friend, was operating the fire monitor and his only deckhand was on the stern of the tug. Soon the stern of the dredge began to slip beneath the surface and water began to pour into the opening I had cut. At this point, the fire monitor was not needed anymore and the tug should have made a quick exit, but the tug was still tied to the dredge. I guess the noise of the tug's engines and the fire monitor drowned out Gary's shouts to the deckhand to untie the tug. I could see Gary screaming over the side of the upper deck and the deckhand sitting on a tow bit looking at the dredge, but not moving. Just as I began to think the tug might join the dredge, I saw the deckhand look up. He jumped into action and cut the line with a fire ax as Gary ran to the wheelhouse and went full throttle ahead. The tug started forward, scraping alongside the dredge while it was sinking. The fire monitor was still spewing a stream of water and washing the top of the dredge's cabin as it moved forward toward the bow. It reached the bow just as the stern hit the bottom of the Gulf and stopped. The dredge poised there as air and water spray spewed out of the forward hatch. That gave the tug just enough time to power clear. The bow slipped beneath the waves and I held my breath hoping and praying the stern didn't reappear on the surface. To my great relief, it stayed there.

 A week later my wife Pamela and I went out with Gene and Eileen to dive the dredge. It had landed upright as planned and we took pictures of ourselves donned in scuba outfits in the wheelhouse. During the dive, I went to the bottom and noticed trails in the sand that looked

Dredge Avocet.

like spoke wheels extending out from the dredge. It was the tracks of hundreds of sea creatures that had made their way toward the dredge, their new home.

CHAPTER 13

Lots of Changes

In 1994, the Alabama reef zone wasn't quite as big as it is now. Although it was huge, it still needed to be bigger. Fuel was cheap and charter boats were sending us up to 50 miles offshore to build reefs. We needed to expand the reef zone to the west. Vernon Minton and the president of the Orange Beach Charter Boat Association met with shrimpers and settled on a large area west of the current zone. It came with conditions. By the end of 1996, cars could no longer be used as reef material. Environmentalists shamed Alabama into prohibiting the use of cars, and I can't honestly disagree with their assessment.

In 1996, no more cars meant I had to make a decision. The new material list for permissible reefs was very limited. It was obvious the reef program was leaning toward structures made of concrete. There were two concrete reef products on the market then: "Reefball" and "Grouper Ghetto." Both were good reef products and the owners would occasionally hire me to deploy them off the *Maranatha*. I was friendly with both owners, but couldn't consider selling any to my customers due to size — or lack thereof. The Reefball, at the time, was only three feet tall and the Grouper Ghetto was five feet tall. These

Reef Making

reefs were popular in Florida and were being deployed by the hundreds as public reefs. They even deployed some for Alabama's charter boats. Within a year, though, you couldn't give a charter boat skipper either of these reefs because their small size limited the production of fish. Their favor in Florida faded as well due to their poor quality as fishing reefs, though they found service in other areas of aquatic needs.

By 1996, I was deploying very large reefs (buses, combines, etc.) and with feedback from the charter fleet, I knew the type, size and shape needed to provide enough fish for everyone on a 30-passenger charter boat. Neither Reefball nor Grouper Ghetto would work for Alabama charter boat fishermen. If I wanted to continue in the reef-building business, I would need a vessel with a crane large enough to carry a very large artificial reef and have deck capacity of at least 150 tons.

I put the cart before the horse and first went after a boat. I applied for a $250,000 Small Business Administration (SBA) loan and began

Coast Guard Buoy Tender Foxglove.

to look for a vessel. I found a 114-foot former Coast Guard buoy tender (*Foxglove*) in Memphis. Built in 1945 and retired from the Coast Guard in the 1960s, it hadn't left the dock in years and served as a quarters boat for a dredging company. It was in bad shape, with paint peeling down in sheets. It had gone through two generator fires in the engine room, destroying the generators and associated wiring. It had three large, antiquated diesel engines (Cleveland inline eight cylinders). The engines and generators were in need of replacement. The entire boat was trashed, and homeless people were living onboard. However, the hull and cabin were sound, and it had never been in saltwater. The owner asked $5,000 for it and for the first time in my life I did not try to negotiate. I sold the engines and transmissions to someone in India for $5,000, getting back the entire purchase price.

It cost more than that to have it towed to Brown Marine shipyard in Orange Beach, which allowed me to do my own work except for the sandblasting and painting. I hired a crew and cut the main cabin off, leaving the wheelhouse, three staterooms, w/two baths and a workshop. That left two open decks, a 30- by 40-foot deck in front of the wheelhouse on the bow and another 30- by 40-footer behind it on the stern. A large galley was under the stern deck.

I removed all the engines and associated equipment. Instead of replacing three engines, I only replaced two. It soon became apparent that my $250,000 was not going to go very far in refitting this vessel. I found two used main engines (12V-71 Detroit diesels) that were refreshed as cheaply as possible. The boat came with a 100KW Caterpillar generator in good condition tucked away in the cargo hold. Also, I recently had sunk a 400-foot-long ship for Escambia County and salvaged a 125KW generator from it. I installed it as the second generator. We tried to repair and reuse as much as possible, but toward the end we had to choose between what we absolutely needed and what could wait until a later date. At the same time, the little *Reefmaker* was running her heart out rushing to deploy as many cars as possible before they were outlawed as of December 31, 1996.

About this time, I purchased another dredge from the same company that owned the *Avocet* and moored it at the same shipyard we were working in. I was hoping to sell it as a reef to a Florida county, but the reef money had dried up. There was a scrap company in Louisiana that offered me $32,000 on delivery. The dredge had a problem. It leaked very badly in just about all the compartments. It needed constant supervision and a dozen or so automatic electric pumps to keep it afloat. I tried to hire several tug companies to deliver it, but once they looked it over, none would touch it.

The original name of my new work vessel was the Coast Guard buoy tender *Foxglove*. I renamed it the *Maranatha*, which means "The Lord Cometh" in Aramaic. (I should mention that my life took a dramatic change when I accepted Jesus as my savior.) With almost no money left, we managed to get the *Maranatha* barely operational. No one in my crew had ever been on a tugboat, much less pushed a barge, including me (except for a very small barge). Nor had I ever operated a vessel of this size (114 feet). But I was running out of money and desperately needed that $32,000.

I hatched a plan. I purchased just enough fuel to make the round trip; it was all I could afford. I parked the *Maranatha* behind the dredge. The bow of the Maranatha contained a ballast tank. I figured if I could fill the ballast tank with water, it should bring the bow down and allow the push knees to mate up to the dredge. As it stood, the push knees towered above the stern of the dredge.

Lots of Changes

Dredge.

However, we couldn't use the ballast tank because the bulkhead was rusted so badly it wouldn't hold water. It was one of those projects that had to wait for repair. This left the bow well above the 2-foot-high stern of the dredge. Consequently, we had to weld a taller framework onto the dredge so we could push it with the *Maranatha*. The dredge was much wider and taller than the *Maranatha* and it was impossible to see over or around it. This type of tow normally would require two tugs: One to pull and steer and the other to push. Since no towing company wanted anything to do with the dredge, that wasn't an option. The dredge had a pilothouse at the front, so we installed a radio and a handheld 12-volt spotlight with a car battery. We hoped this arrangement would allow people in the dredge to give steering directions via radio to the *Maranatha* so it could navigate channels and buoys along the way. Because the *Maranatha* had plenty of generator power, I purchased a lot of extension cords and ran power from the *Maranatha* to all the preexisting electric bilge pumps all over the

Reef Making

dredge. In addition, I ran power to the dredge's wheelhouse for a battery charger to maintain power to their radio and spotlight.

It was January and our journey would take us west on the ICW and out into Mobile Bay via Bon Secour Bay channel. We would cross the Mobile Ship Channel, enter the Heron channel leading under the Dauphin Island Bridge and continue into the Mississippi Sound. Mobile Bay and the Mississippi Sound were open bodies of water, but they had some narrow channels in places. Given the dredge's badly deteriorated hull and our inexperience, any high winds would make the dredge uncontrollable and could push it out of the channel and aground in high seas. Such a scenario would spell disaster for us. The fragile dredge hull would break apart and as a result I would be consulting a bankruptcy attorney before I got back to land.

After we transited the Sound, we would enter The Rigolets canal, which led to the lock on the Mississippi River in New Orleans. Reaching that canal would be a relief as it provided the only protection from wind or heavy seas after entering Mobile Bay. Due to our unfamiliarity with locks and the Mississippi, I didn't want to deal with either, considering the highly controlled procedures overseen by the Coast Guard and vicious currents that exceeded my experience.

Per our agreement with the scrap company, we were to deliver the dredge to the lock and the company's crew would take over from there. The entire distance we needed to travel was about 150 nautical miles, 77 of which would be across open water. We estimated 27 hours running time to The Rigolets' protective entrance and 12 more hours to the lock on the Mississippi River. We didn't want to arrive there at night, so we timed our departure for 3 a.m., which would put us at The Rigolets canal at sunrise 30 hours away.

Lots of Changes

Everything proceeded as planned until about 15 miles into the trip, when one of the engines developed a serious oil leak. We shut it down and ran on one engine. I hired a man named Bill Douglas of Michigan. He was a genius when it came to working on mechanical equipment. Bill never worked on a large vessel before. Even so, he managed to fashion a patch to stop the leak. Not more than an hour later the swells from the Gulf of Mexico coming through the mouth of Mobile Bay began to rock both the dredge and the Maranatha. It broke our special framework for pushing the dredge. Fortunately, we had brought along a welding machine and after limping through the area of swells, Bill patched up the broken pieces.

We forgot to take coffee with us, so as we passed under the Dauphin Island Bridge, we had a local friend drop a can of coffee off the bridge as we passed under it. We began to gain some confidence as time went on, but even that didn't last in the darkness. We had the little jury-rigged handheld spotlight, but it paled in comparison to the real spotlight on the *Maranatha*. However, the latter's spotlight was no use for looking ahead, due to the bulk of the dredge in front of it. It was difficult to locate buoys, but I did have a new GPS with a built-in chart and that proved to be a lifesaver. It could get me to the next buoy, and the guys in the dredge's wheelhouse would then guide us safely past the buoy until it came into view of the *Maranatha's* spotlight. It was nerve-wracking work, especially when passing another tug/barge combination coming from the opposite direction in the narrow channel at night. We struggled on, however, and God must have been looking out for us with calm seas and light winds.

As dawn approached, we could see the mouth of The Rigolets. Soon we were passing through the entrance and into a protected canal of calm water. No sooner had we entered our safe haven then the wind

Reef Making

began to blow 30 knots out of the northwest. If that had happened two hours sooner, the outcome of this story would probably have been entirely different.

The rest of the trip was uneventful and at sundown we were nosing up to the bank just outside the Industrial Lock to the Mississippi River. We spent the night there and celebrated our success. The next morning the scrapyard tugs took the dredge off our hands and we headed home with a check for $32,000. On the way back, due to 30 knot winds, we encountered some of the roughest weather I've ever experienced in the 20 years I've sailed on the *Maranatha*. The boat rolled mercilessly because it had no ballast water and almost no fuel. Also, since the refitting of the *Maranatha* was not complete, lots of things were not permanently installed and the violent rolling motion dislodged everything not fastened down.

The pilot's chair was mounted on a heavy platform, but not bolted to the floor. The chair, file cabinets, portable heaters, boxes of supplies, charts and bottles all dislodged and made a continuous trek back and forth across the wheelhouse deck. The binnacle (compass) was not secured either, so I draped myself across the steering station, and with both arms embraced the large ship's binnacle, I salvaged from a ship. As the boat rolled, I would lift my legs as the chair and other debris passed by. Bruce Tabor, a friend who came along to help, went into a cabin. He rolled into a bunk, thinking he was safe there. Unfortunately, the bunk was just sitting on top of an old military desk. During a particularly bad roll, he found himself underneath the bunk that was sliding back and forth across the cabin. Many hours later we entered the calm Intracoastal Canal in Alabama and were safely home.

CHAPTER 14

Hard Times

At that point I had the perfect reef-building vessel. Though still not quite finished, it was usable (it would take another 10 years to complete the *Maranatha*). Now, I needed a reef to sell. For some reason I didn't think that would be a problem. I had a scheme in mind, but it didn't work out the way I figured it would. I thought building a concrete reef would be simple. I found out otherwise. I learned what other concrete builders already knew. Small concrete structures are easy to build; large concrete structures are not. Large concrete structures are very expensive to build, very heavy and extremely difficult to transport and deploy. The *Maranatha* had a 20-ton crane, but a rolling sea can produce moments of stress to a crane that far exceed its land-rated capacity. So, in reality, the limit of our 20-ton crane was only about 5 tons.

My customers were used to spending $250 on a car, but a large concrete structure equal to a car in reef value would weigh over five tons and cost upwards of $3,000. That and the severe limits on red snapper imposed by National Oceanic and Atmospheric Administration (NOAA) Fisheries and the Gulf of Mexico Fishery Management Council, plus a general lack of interest in any reef other than a car, made for a dismal future for my new vessel and me. Then I came across a concrete pipe company in Mobile that accumulated a lot of defective pipes in its manufacturing process. When I talked with the head honcho, I was informed the company would give me all the rejected pipes I wanted if I paid for the trucking costs, which were reasonable. It seemed like the answer to my problem.

The *Maranatha* was too large to dock at Earl's Marina. So, I had to find another place to keep it. We located an abandoned shipyard in bankruptcy on the ICW at Plash Island near the entrance to Mobile Bay. We began to take reef orders for concrete pipe. A truck would dump the pipes next to the boat and we would load them on deck. The pipes were heavy, some nearing our limit of five tons. The weight and difficulty in handling drove the price higher than I liked and orders were few. Later we discovered that small batches of concrete pipes did not make good reef material and all our customers complained about the lack of fish. As a result, I abandoned the use of concrete pipe as a viable replacement for cars. We could still use school buses and I could sell them easily. The problem was finding them in the first place.

In 1984, I purchased a small seaplane (Lake Amphibian) and learned how to fly it. I used it as part of my vessel repair servicing the Tennessee-Tombigbee (Tenn-Tom) Waterway. Later, when I sold the shipyard, I kept the plane because I loved to fly. I still have a Lake Amphibian and fly it regularly. In those days, I used the plane in my search for reef material. I flew around at low altitudes looking behind every house or on every farm for any type of bus. If I found one, I would note the location, drive over later and offer to purchase it. Getting the buses from their resting places to the *Reefmaker* was not easy. For years they sat there on rotten tires, with trees growing through wheel wells, engine compartments and every other opening.

We evicted various types of animals and reptiles and disposed of tons of trash that had been stored inside. We had to make each bus safe enough to tow and sink as a permitted reef.

I needed some sort of wrecker to drag the buses out from their resting places and transport them over the road. At an auction I purchased a 2-ton truck with a winch and transformed it into a wrecker of sorts. My best source of buses came from two companies that sold and rented school buses in Theodore, west of Mobile and about an hour away. If they had an old bus that needed to be retired, they would strip it of the engine, transmission, lights and other recyclable parts and leave two wheels on the back or front so I could lift the other end and tow it back to Orange Beach. Most of the time I just hooked on to the front of the bus, but sometimes I had to tow one from the back with the front axle and wheels serving as rolling support.

The Marantha *loaded down with school buses destined to become fishing reefs.*

I towed buses many times without mishap, but there was one time when things didn't go well, and it burned into my memory as especially unforgettable. In Mobile I picked up a school bus with wheels on the front and none on the rear. I hoisted the rear of the bus with the winch and secured it with some chains.

I began my eastbound trip on I-10, passing through the tunnel under the Mobile River and across the Bay Way, and exited southbound on Hwy 59 toward Orange Beach. All was uneventful until I reached Gulf Shores and turned onto the Canal Road next to the Intracoastal Canal leading to Orange Beach. I was cruising along, when I heard an explosion. I looked in the rear-view mirror in time to see a large locking ring depart from one of the tires and begin rolling toward oncoming traffic. A bus locking ring is heavy enough to do considerable damage to a car. I watched in horror as the ring passed one car, narrowly missing the car's left rear side. It continued crossing the opposing lane of traffic while angling toward the canal. It crossed in front of a second car and just missed it before bouncing up and landing in the water.

I pulled over, got out and went back to see what happened. The tire had blown out. The locking ring that secures the tire had come off, though the flat tire was still on the rim. (This particular locking ring system was abandoned by the tire industry years ago because of the many deaths the rings caused during tire repairs.) I was only about 6 miles from my storage yard. Since I didn't care whether the tire or rim were damaged running on a flat tire, maybe I could keep going on the flat until I reached my destination.

I hopped back into the truck and set off again. All went well for about 3 more miles, when I felt a jerk. I looked in the rear-view mirror

Hard Times

and saw dust and dirt fly off the area of the flat tire. It felt like someone had slammed on the brakes in the bus. So, I pulled over again.

Upon inspection, I found the tie rod had broken. It's the contraption that connects both front wheels to keep them going in the same direction. The good wheel was fine, tracking straight ahead, but the flat tire wheel had turned 90 degrees to the direction of travel. In short, one wheel wanted to go straight and the other wanted to turn left. This made everything more complicated. Before this latest catastrophe, I could have dropped the bus on the side of the road, driven to the yard, found a good tire and wheel, returned and changed the tire. Now, the whole bus would have to be lifted onto a trailer for the final three miles to the yard. And I didn't have a trailer big enough to handle the bus.

I closely examined the situation and reviewed my options. The bottom of the steps, where children enter and exit the bus, was touching the pavement and supporting a lot of the weight. The tire that had skidded sideways on the pavement was supporting the rest. I looked to see if the skidding steps and tire had damaged the pavement. Amazingly, other than a black skid mark, there was no sign of any damage. What if I could drag the whole thing skidding on the steps and flat tire the last three miles home? I decided to try; after all, what did I have to lose? I hopped back into the truck and got everything moving again. I was amazed the truck could pull it, so amazed I decided to find out how fast it would go. After all, the faster I got home, the better. This sort of attitude turned out to be a mistake, but I was able to get the truck to 40 mph and figured I had seen the last of my problems.

I think God must have a great sense of humor, especially when it comes to me. What happened next was so implausible that it could only be explained as a supernatural event. Who would suspect that two simultaneous events, so remote and seemingly unrelated, could combine to create an incident that transformed a minor mishap into a spectacle?

As I barreled down Canal Road, I was so proud of my truck's ability to reach 40 mph dragging a wheelless school bus down the road with ease, that I never gave a thought about the correlation of friction and speed to heat.

My face, heretofore swelling with pride, suddenly changed to wearing a look of shock. Sonic booms are rare, and I can't remember when I last heard one, but never in a million years would the timing be so perfectly coordinated to a non-related event. The sonic boom shook Orange Beach, rattling windows and shaking buildings; surely, a Navy jet based at the Pensacola Naval Air Station must have generated it.

As it turned out, however, I — not some fighter pilot — would get the blame in Orange Beach. Who could have known that at the same moment of a sonic boom the bus would burst into flames? I am not blaming the fire on the sonic boom. The sonic boom merely caused everyone on Canal Road either to look outside or come out of the various shops and businesses to see what had happened.

Their concern was not unwarranted. What they saw was a school bus enveloped in flames. They saw black smoke bellowing off that flattened tire as the vehicle went by, dragged along by a truck with the name *Reefmaker* painted on it. Of course, most everyone thought I had caused the explosion, which shook and rattled buildings and their contents.

I was now the subject of great amusement or horror, depending on who was looking. The black smoke and burning paint bellowing off the hood area of the bus completely obscured the road behind me.

I realized I had a very serious problem. Old school buses have wooden floors covered in rubber mats and foam seats that are highly combustible. Then there was the gas tank, just a few feet away from the burning tire. All in all, and including the complicated attachment system I employed to tow the bus, stopping just then would encourage a doomsday event. If I stopped, the flames would quickly envelop the bus before I could unhook chains and lower the burning hulk with the winch, undo more chains and get away. I would not only lose my investment in the bus, but my truck would become part of a huge, smoldering black spot on the side of the road. It seemed to me that by continuing to move the flames were likely to spew out the back away from the combustible material inside the bus and hopefully only burn the tire, fender and hood area. All I could do was keep moving to avoid a much larger fire that would blaze up if I stopped. What was needed was a water hose. As I drove, I tried to recall who had a readily available water hose in Orange Beach. I couldn't remember if Sam's gas station had a hose, but then it occurred to me that probably that establishment wouldn't appreciate me pulling in next to the gas pumps with a burning bus. I supposed the better thing to do was head for the fire department.

I was pedal to the metal, still doing 40 mph and passing people standing by the road, some waving, some looking aghast with hands over their mouths. I kept glancing in my rear-view mirror, trying to gauge if the fire was moving forward toward my truck. I watched a car emerge from the black smoke at a high rate of speed. It was a station wagon. I watched as it accelerated past the flames, weaving erratically in the left lane, until it overtook me. A middle-aged couple was in the front seat and two children occupied the rear seat. The station wagon pulled alongside of me and the woman rolled her window down and

Reef Making

screamed, "Your bus is on fire!" I nodded politely and said, "I know." This caused each of them to exhibit puzzled expressions. They pulled ahead and kept going. A minute passed and a police car emerged from the smoke with blue lights flashing. As he came alongside, the officer used hand motions to indicate I was to stop right then and there. I shook my head and yelled, "I'm going to the fire department." In case he only understood hand signals, I pointed ahead with my hand and never backed off the accelerator. He rolled his window down and yelled for me to pull over. Again, I repeated, "I'm going to the fire department," pointed my finger again in that direction and kept on driving. I can't say if he actually heard me, but he fell back beyond the smoke and I kept going, full throttle.

Finally, a couple of miles later, the fire department came into view. In fact, it was only a block farther down the road than the *Reefmaker* yard. Though it is no longer there, at the time the fire department was located on the corner of Canal Road and Walker Lane. I quickly turned onto the dirt road facing the fire department, pulled to a stop and looked toward the doors. They were closed and then I remembered that it was a volunteer fire department and no one was likely to be there. I looked to see if perhaps there was a garden hose attached to the building. There wasn't. My fate seemed sealed, as there was no place to turn around. My destiny was now in the hands of volunteer firemen and their ability to deliver a quick response. The police car, with its blue lights still flashing, had followed me and was parked a safe distance away. I could see the officer talking on the radio. I jumped out and looked back toward the bus. Amazingly, the fire had burned itself out. The only evidence that there had ever been a fire was the smoldering hot metal it left behind.

Hard Times

I could hear the volunteers coming, as their personal vehicles were equipped with sirens. Trucks and cars pulled up haphazardly. Their drivers jumped out and ran into the firehouse. Moments later the doors sprang open and the fire engine roared out, narrowly missing the bus and me. The engine then pulled onto Canal Road and headed back from where I came from. The police officer backed up, turned around and followed the fire truck down Canal Road.

I was left there to ponder the situation. It seems that the burning tire under the bus spewed chunks of burning rubber along the side of the road. It being a dry season, many small, inconsequential roadside fires flared up. It was the reason the firemen ignored me and headed back down Canal Road to put out the flames, which they did quickly. I never heard from the policeman again. Maybe Orange Beach didn't have an ordinance against towing burning buses.

Wiser from the experience, I went on about my business. The bus was transported to the Walter Marine yard using a second winch truck going in reverse and holding up the front of the bus. We continued to use buses until the ADCNR outlawed them as reef material.

As it turns out, buses, semis, vans, railroad cars and New York subway cars all have a basic glitch. The rivets used to construct these vehicles are of a different and weaker type of metal than the sheets they hold. Therein lies a problem. When dissimilar metals that are connected together come in contact with saltwater, a process called galvanic corrosion occurs. The lesser metal will dissolve and the more seaworthy one will attract the properties of the lesser. Thus, rivets will dissolve before anything else and the entire structure will collapse like a house of cards. This usually takes about three or four years, which is enough time to turn a bus into a private reef worth the money.

Reef Making

Subway cars.

CHAPTER 15

NOAA

Looking back, I could not have picked a worse time to invest in the artificial reef business. Despite indications to the contrary, like most other fishermen I thought that the current superior fishing economy would continue forever.

By 1990, most fishermen with any experience realized that red snapper should be managed. The days when a boat could bring back hundreds of pounds of snapper to the dock without putting a dent in the population were approaching their end. More and more fishermen meant that catches needed to be curtailed. When NOAA's National Marine Fisheries Service (NMFS) announced it was going to manage red snapper, most fishermen welcomed them with open arms. They wanted to see a healthy fishery for their children and grandchildren to enjoy.

In 1990 the NMFS imposed a seven-fish bag limit, a 13-inch length limit and a 360-day season for red snapper on recreational fishermen in the federal zone. The Orange Beach Charter Boat Association welcomed the ruling and voted to recommend that an inch be added to the length limit, imposing a 14-inch length on its members as a show of good faith. It was a reasonable limit that everyone could live with.

And it worked; from 1990 to 1994, fishermen noticed an increase in red snapper and expected NMFS to announce the same results. NMFS didn't. Instead, it declared the biomass of snapper was still decreasing and by 1995 they decreased the daily bag limit to five and increased the size limit to 15 inches. The fishing season remained open year-round. Fishermen continued to notice an increase in the snapper population, but each year the NMFS put more restrictive catch limits and seasons on red snapper. The limits continued to decrease until they got as low as two fish (2008) and the seasons decreased to as little as 3 days.

In 1996 I ignored all the warning signs and expanded my business as the snapper fishery regulations began to bite into the incomes of all those who depended on it. Charter boats, homes and pickup trucks were being foreclosed on. The charter fleet began to decrease. Who could blame a fisherman for not paying for an artificial reef for three days of fishing and only a couple of fish per person?

Many of us wondered how the NMFS could not see that the snapper biomass was increasing. Snapper biomass began to explode again. Historically, red snapper only flourished in the northern Gulf of Mexico. But then the population increased to the point that the fish were impacting other reef species. Red snapper are ravenous fish, eating anything, including their own. As they began to consume other species, once considered to be in healthy numbers, suddenly those species needed protection. In a nutshell, the National Marine Fisheries Service's science was severely defective, and the fishery was being mismanaged. At one meeting, even a NMFS scientist admitted the science was flawed and later others at NMFS confessed as much, but never made any real attempts to correct the flaws.

To put the problem and solution in simple layman's terms, in the beginning NMFS tried to determine three factors as a basis for managing the fishery:

1. How many red snapper are supposed to be in the Gulf of Mexico (historically)?
2. How many are there at present?
3. How many can be caught each year while still rebuilding the population?

Those are easy questions to ask, but not easy questions to answer. Back then, NMFS had a budget of $900 million to monitor the fishery, and people thought that the NMFS surely could overcome the difficulties associated with accurate appraisals of the northern Gulf's snapper population. As it eventually turned out, the agency's methods, results and generally negative effects on that fishery could not have been worse had they been done intentionally.

So, how many red snapper are supposed to be in the Gulf? If you go with real historical records before oil platforms and artificial reefs came along, the population was very small; in fact, tiny compared to what it was in 1990. So, the fish managers decided to go with population numbers extrapolated by counting all the oil platforms and artificial reefs. I don't know how they did this — maybe with historical records of landings, but with the methods NMFS used, there was no way for it to be accurate and complete.

NMFS got its base number of fish based upon the entire fish population of the northern Gulf, including the population brought about by the installation of oil platforms and artificial reefs that provided favorable habitat for the red snappers and caused their population

Reef Making

to increase. They used this number as the historic population count for red snapper. Then they proceeded to try to count the present red snapper population. However, the method they used didn't count the snapper on artificial reefs where they lived, but searched for them in areas where they don't live, on flat sandy bottom. This caused their studies to severely underestimate the current red snapper population. (You can't make this stuff up!) The NMFS sampling method involved taking four cameras to a place of pure sandy bottom with no natural or artificial reefs. Then the cameras were lowered to the bottom and, after a few hours, they were pulled up. Finally, any red snapper that swam by and were caught on film were counted. This was all a big joke to fishermen, who know that red snapper only live on structure and not on a plain sandy bottom.

I watched Congressman Bradley Byrne (R-AL) question Samuel Rauch III of NOAA on Dec. 4, 2014, in a Congressional hearing regarding why NOAA/NMFS don't sample for red snapper on structure (www.youtube.com/watch?time_continue=14&v=hcLUbeoja5w). To paraphrase his reply: "Red snapper don't live exclusively on structure and the reason we don't sample for red snapper on structure is because we might damage our sampling gear."

Okay, now close your mouth; it gets worse.

I had seen the vessel they used to do the sampling and my son knows the captain, so as ridiculous as it seems, what Rauch said was true. In effect the captain rode around a location and, using sophisticated sonar, made sure there were no artificial reefs within a half-mile. Once he had determined the bottom was pure sand with no structure, he dropped the cameras to count red snapper.

The next question NMFS tried to determine was how many red snapper were caught on average. It tried a lot of methods. Getting records of every boat licensed in each state and adding the bag limit to each boat was one of them. No distinction was made whether it was a ski boat, sport fisherman, bass boat or jet ski. NMFS counted each licensed boat as catching a snapper limit each day of the season. To make this methodology even more bizarre, the agency continued the count even during and after hurricanes, when no fishing was taking place. Of course, the result was that too many red snapper were being caught. Conclusion: Stricter limits were needed.

When the fishermen complained, NMFS put people at marinas and boat ramps to ask people how many red snapper they caught that day. Good idea, but for some reason they knocked off at 3 p.m. each day and went home before most of the fishermen returned. Conclusion: No red snapper were caught, so stricter seasons were needed.

NMFS spent a lot of money hiring folks from northern universities who had never seen a red snapper to produce a computer program to determine seasons, bag limits and sizes. They also handed over the flawed data collected on flat sandy bottom to the universities. To make matters worse, the universities took three and a half years to get the data into computers. Bag limits, lengths and seasons were determined by three-and-a-half-year-old, flawed data. Frustration, bewilderment on our part? You bet.

When Gulf fishermen and even state officials complained about the ridiculous mismanagement and offered real contradictory data collected by each state's universities and conservation and natural resources departments with verifiable results, NMFS rejected the data. Instead, it continued to use useless, corrupted and outdated data. This total disregard for an accurate assessment frustrated state governments to the point of rebellion.

Reef Making

Florida and Texas are the only two Gulf states with territorial waters extending nine nautical miles. The state waters of the other Gulf states (Alabama, Mississippi and Louisiana) extend 3 nautical miles offshore. This became a problem for NMFS. The mismanagement got so bad that Texas set its own limits within its 9-mile limit. It began building artificial reefs in state waters and basically told the NMFS to shove it. Florida has followed suit at times, but felt bad when NMFS answered by subtracting Texas' and Florida's estimated catch over their allotted amount from Alabama, Mississippi and Louisiana, which made our seasons much shorter.

Whether it was intentional or not, NMFS set the yearly biomass quota very low and invited the user groups to fight over it. Recreational, charter and commercial groups spend all their time fighting with each other, rather than banding together and confronting NMFS.

Defining the problem and finding a workable solution wasn't that difficult then or now, until a lot of bureaucrats, computer geeks and young, inexperienced marine scientists got involved. The result demonstrates the wisdom of the old saying, "Keep it simple, stupid."

It's not that complicated. Forget how many historical snapper are supposed to be there. We don't need to know that. Forget how many are being landed on the docks. We don't need to know that, either.

We have the technology and expertise to use special remotely operated vehicles (ROVs) with cameras to study fish populations and range of sizes on artificial reefs. The solution would be to extend each state's fishing authority to 50 miles offshore and allow them to license and control seasons, bag limits and size limits in their respective states. Texas already does this. Have NOAA give the states some of that $900 million budget — or whatever it is now — for vessels and ROV equipment for continuous monitoring. Actual reef sizes and the number of snapper on them could be used to establish an accurate baseline. Correlate that information with a reasonable guesstimate of the size and number of unstudied artificial reefs and oil and gas platforms and you can get an accurate picture of the current biomass of red snapper in that particular state's territory.

Keep the sampling going year-round and feed the data into a computer program weekly to determine whether biomass stock is increasing, decreasing or remaining the same. Adjust bag limits, sizes and seasons on a regular basis to rebuild the stock to whatever level seems appropriate for that state. Then control it with harvest limits, size limits and seasons. We have used similar methods for years to manage deer populations, with great success.

Almost all marine scientists agree that artificial reefs increase red snapper biomass. Given the application of a common-sense approach to fishery management, states could build more artificial reefs to increase their biomass and therefore increase their fishing effort. States that don't want to go through the bother would have the option of doing nothing, and they also could watch revenues in the form of fishing licenses and tourist dollars go to adjacent states. It wouldn't take long for all the states to get on board; besides, no politician can stand to see a tax dollar drift away that otherwise could land in his state.

Theory, an unproven idea? Hardly; this management method based on hard science is not a fantasy. Using a Remotely Operated Vehicle (ROV), Dr. Bob Shipp conducted a study of Alabama's reef zone that followed the protocol previously mentioned. Dr. Shipp, who ran the University of South Alabama's Marine Science Department for many years, was able to determine an accurate biomass figure for the state's reef zone. The results of his extensive study showed that Ala-

Reef Making

bama, with its 1.5 percent of the Gulf of Mexico coastline, has more red snapper in its artificial reef zone than NMFS says exists in the entire Gulf of Mexico.

My point is this: If NMFS was really focused on saving the red snapper from overharvest, it would have paid more attention to Alabama's model of privately managed artificial reefs and encouraged other states to adopt similar management systems. What if states encouraged fishermen to build private reefs and gave them special access to some of the fish they helped raise through their sweat and money? It's not rocket science; if you have a field of corn to feed 100 people and it's not enough, NMFS's solution would be to limit the consumption of corn. Anyone else with the sense the Almighty gave a Billy goat would just plant a second field of corn.

The only hope for the future is to turn over the management of the fishery to those who know it best: the states and the fishing groups that use it. We already have the tools in place to make that happen. Things are slowly changing and, hopefully, NOAA/NMFS will allow states to police their own fisheries, without dictating any limits.

CHAPTER 16

Struggling to Survive

In 1996, thanks to NMFS's suffocating harvest rules, private reef building almost ground to a halt. Faced with a large note payment every month, I struggled to find something to do with the *Maranatha* to pay the bills. Then I noticed that there was a lot of activity going on across from Brown's on the ICW at Reynolds Concrete Plant. Odebrecht Construction Company was building bridge sections there for transport to Garcon Point 32 miles away in Gulf Breeze, Florida. I inquired if there was need of another vessel. Thus, we were hired to transport barge loads of bridge material from Orange Beach to Garcon Point. Fortunately for me, Odebrecht is known for its frugality and paid more attention to what I would charge than to my qualifications. I learned as I went. The bridge took about three years to complete. I worked for the company for two and a half years. During that time, I used off-days to keep the reef business alive. My competitor, Steve, was seeing a decline in his reef business as well. He was making reefs from chicken cages, which were 4 feet by 8 feet by 5 feet and were used to transport chickens on trucks. The snapper regulations eventually forced him out of business.

Reef Making

Six months before the contract with Odebrecht ended, I began to search for something else to do. Reef building alone was not going to keep the bills paid. During the previous two years, through trial and error, I had learned a lot about tug boating. Some of it involved hard lessons: What to do when you lose both rudders, what to do when you run aground, what to do when the engine room catches fire and what to do if you become detached from the barge in Pensacola Pass and your barge is carried out into the Gulf with an outgoing tide. By the end of those two and half years, I had become very experienced in barge handling.

I began to look for tugboat work, first locally, then as far as a hundred miles away, and then anywhere. No one needed the *Maranatha*. As we got closer to the end of the job with Odebrecht, I began to pray for something so I could continue to pay my bills. Then one day the phone rang. It was the U.S. Navy in Panama City. It had a pair of 130-foot vessels used for diver training, but two new replacement vessels were on the way and there wasn't enough dock space for all four. The Navy offered the vessels for reefs to any Florida government agency that wanted them, but no one had the funds necessary for cleanup and deployment. So, the Navy turned to me. Would I be interested in cleaning and deploying the vessels somewhere close by for free? In exchange, I could salvage all

YDT 14 *and* 15.

Struggling to Survive

equipment off the vessels and collect $28,000 in cash for towing. I took this as an answer to prayer. I called Eileen and offered the vessels to Escambia County for free. She was thrilled and obtained an affirmative answer within 24 hours. The vessels, *YDT 14* and *15*, were in perfect condition and carried lots of machinery, decompression chambers, air compressors, etc.

The abandoned shipyard I was using for dock space had been sold for condos, but I found another place to rent on the ICW just west of the Hwy 59 bridge in Gulf Shores. Once that was settled, we towed the first YDT to our new dock. Months later we towed the second YDT to the dock. Then, I placed an ad in *Boats & Harbors* offering to sell the equipment onboard the vessels. There was no timeline for the deployment, and I was able to support my business through the sale of items off the vessels for more than two years. The vessels were eventually deployed offshore from Escambia County without incident.

Was this an answer to prayer or merely a coincidence? I had to know. After I sank the vessels, I called my Navy contact and he directed me to the person in charge of retired Navy vessels. I asked if more vessels were available. The answer was an emphatic "NO," and furthermore, he said, my getting the two vessels wasn't supposed to have happened. He added that I had a legitimate contract, but he couldn't explain how it came about. Navy vessels destined for retirement are supposed to go through a long and rigorous process and be towed to Maryland and stored in a fleet. Only then can a vessel be acquired for a reef program, according to him. The process takes years and any useful equipment removed still belongs to the Navy. Finally, he said that even though my acquisition of the vessels was legal, he hoped no one ever found out about it and promised it would never happen again. My conclusion: Prayer works.

CHAPTER 17

New Reef Design and Florida

About this time, I attempted to design and build a concrete igloo-type reef, using a shotcrete gun. It's a device that sprays concrete onto a wire mesh frame. The guns are used to build swimming pools. I found out it was impossible to regulate the weight to produce a consistent reef unit. It was difficult to build, impossible to stack on deck and very heavy. It was expensive, which would not work for my customers. I tried different configurations, shapes and sizes. I rejected them all for one reason or another and gave up on shotcrete.

The goal was to produce relatively inexpensive, yet sizable, reefs. As I searched for answers, my mind kept going back to the seed of an idea. There was one item that was readily available for free and used with success by other reef builders: old tires. However, it was a controversial solution and I had to think about it long and hard. My German ancestry required a non-emotional black-and-white analysis. I was raised to question everything and make decisions based on facts instead of what the current social climate seemed to be. The use of automobile tires as reef material had its proponents and opponents. There was no consensus and people had varying perspectives. On

Reef Making

the negative side, making reefs from automobile tires might suggest dumping trash in the ocean to get rid of them. Our oceans are not landfills. No one wants to think of diving in pristine waters only to find a bunch of old tires strewn about. Added to that, worn-out tires constitute one of the most problematic disposal challenges known to man and we certainly don't want them in our oceans. The detractors had seemingly good arguments.

Once you get past the general societal view of tires being potential nuisances to the marine environment, however, there are other considerations. Tires are totally safe for the marine environment. Although not the best reef material, they make an acceptable substrate for marine life. Their only problem is their neutral buoyancy in water and their unknown lifespans. New Jersey used tires as reef material for many years with great success. Its fishery managers developed a formula for a concrete-to-tire ratio that kept them anchored in place even during storm events. New Jersey's tire-to-reef program was eventually abandoned, not because it wasn't successful, but due to the negative attitude toward using tires as reefs. However, John Winn of the Corps of Engineers was a big proponent of tire reefs. Every time I visited him in his Mobile office, he would pull out a model of New Jersey's tire reef and encourage me to give it a try.

New Jersey embedded the tire standing up in a block of concrete. Once a tire was covered in marine life it was no longer an eyesore, but a beautiful living, breathing habitat for marine life. However, New Jersey's method of anchoring tires limited the height of the reef to the diameter of a standing tire. By Alabama standards, that wasn't tall enough to make a decent reef. Opponents of tire reefs will display an old tire removed from the ocean bottom and comment on the lack of marine growth. This is due to the close proximity to the ocean floor.

Elevate the tire a few feet above the bottom and marine growth will cover the tire. Usually a reef will sink into the sand between a few inches and up to two feet, depending on its design, weight and the depth of water in which it was deployed. The shallower the water, the more the reef subsides into the bottom. I needed something at least 8 feet tall to produce the amount of fish my customers were used to.

Given that I was stuck and in need of material that would produce a big and relatively inexpensive reef unit, I decided to heed John Winn's encouragement. Since tires are harmless to the marine environment, that was a big plus. However, to use tires as reef material properly and responsibly, I needed a way to ensure that they stayed in one place for the life of a tire, which is unknown. Concrete was the logical answer. The Romans invented concrete more than 2,000 years ago and their structures are still standing, so I knew it would be an ideal material for the tires. Designwise, I had the idea of a concrete tetrahedron made of concrete beams with tires strung on the beams. Further, the concrete tetrahedron needed to meet or exceed the weight requirements New Jersey developed for its tire reefs and be strong enough to survive storm events.

I had a reef customer who owned a machine shop in Saraland, Alabama. I showed him my drawing and he offered to design and build the molds, plus construct the reefs. I took him up on his offer. The result was a reef that stood 10 feet tall, with each beam containing 10 tires for a total of 60 tires. The ratio of concrete-to-tire was twice as much as the New Jersey formula called for. I presented the reef design to Alabama officials and they required that it be thoroughly tested for a year to make sure it didn't move or break apart. We built a few prototypes and deployed them for study. Dr. Shipp supervised the study and a year later pronounced that the new tire reef was stable and

Reef Making

Tire reef.

approved for use. Twenty-two years later the tire reefs our company deployed then are still intact and producing fish.

I was able to sell the new reef unit for $850 deployed, which was a reasonable price. They caught on, and soon we were making regular treks up the Mobile River to Saraland, and loading 40 tire reef units on the boat at a time. We would then make our way back down the river, through Mobile and back to our dock in Gulf Shores. The ADCNR would issue permits and soon the tire reefs were on the bottom, maturing into marine habitat. The reefs lived up to expectations and orders began to flow in.

One of my customers was Dr. Edwin Roberts of Pensacola. He was an avid diver and fisherman. He discovered the new tire reefs were havens for lobsters. In addition, each reef produced an abundance of triggerfish, red snapper and other species. By the year 2000, we had deployed more than 3,000 tire reefs in Alabama with no problems. I thought my new tire reef would be an innovation to reef building everywhere. I even obtained a patent for it.

In 1999, Roberts became the first chairman of the newly formed Florida Fish and Wildlife Conservation Commission (FWC). The FWC took control of artificial reefs from the Florida DEP. Roberts was a private reef builder and was so impressed with Alabama's Reef Program that he took other FWC Commissioners fishing in Alabama and convinced them of the many benefits private reefs provided. The Commissioners were duly impressed and agreed it was time to obtain Corps of Engineers' permits for large reef areas in Florida that mimicked Alabama's Reef Program. In addition, Roberts wanted to deploy 10 of my tire reefs for a study to explore its possible use in Florida. However, over the next year, Roberts' plan and my tire reef became the targets of some of the most radical, unintelligent, ill-advised, and unreasonable people I have ever had the misfortune to be in contact with.

When it was all over, and the dust cleared, I used the Freedom of Information Act to obtain copies of more than 1,000 emails of individuals in several governmental agencies who used their low-level positions and membership in "Public Employees for Environmental Responsibility" (PEER) to distort facts, withhold information and manipulate the system to their advantage. The individual who led their crusade, now deceased, manipulated his superiors and fellow employees, used his network of PEER members to submit untruths that discredited my reef and contravened the Florida Fish and Wildlife Commissioners' wishes. Why? Before he worked for the government, he worked for my competitor.

It's a long story, but it began with the Florida offices of the Army Corps of Engineers. Florida has a "different" Corps of Engineers than Alabama does. One would think all Corps policies would be the same. That's not the case; each Corps has its own personality. The Florida Corps is vehemently opposed to large permitted areas as the following quote from one of the recovered emails I have in my possession states (quotes my emphasis): *"Right now our policy has been to potentially reauthorize existing large area reefs,* [which is considered to be seven by seven miles — tiny by Alabama standards] *but deny or reduce the size of new large area reefs coming in."*

In addition, the emails revealed a very negative attitude toward private reefs. An Alabama-style reef program overlaid in Florida waters was doomed from the start. There were forces working behind the scenes, manipulating the outcome before the process even got underway. The first nail in the coffin was the "30-day comment period," not required, but used by the Corps to kill projects.

In bureaucratic terms, a comment period is essentially a complaint box for receiving public comments. As the comments arrive at the Corps office, the project petitioners can offer counter comments. At the end of the comment period, the Corps is supposed to make a just decision based on the comments and answers to the comments. However, Corps employees can influence the 30-day comment period to reflect any result they want. I have a forwarded email from a Corps decision maker to Florida DEP officials voicing his pre-opposition to tire reefs even before the comment period was finished.

Some comments voiced legitimate concerns, but a lot were knee-jerk reactions that had no scientific basis. Many of those referenced

New Reef Design and Florida

a couple of examples of problems associated with tires in the early days of reef building. In one instance, a bundle of tires was cabled together and deployed off North Carolina's coast in 35 feet of water. The steel cable rusted and parted, and left the tires to drift away in the marine environment. Next, a hurricane came up the coast and loose tires wound up on the beach. The same thing happened in south Florida, except the tires wound up on a coral reef. Both deployments were doomed to fail from the get-go, causing environmental harm that unjustly tainted tires as poor reef material.

I tried to respond to comments with factual information and solid assurances of my reef's stability, which involved reports of thorough testing by Alabama marine biologists, records of thousands of successful deployments in Alabama, plus a report on the many years of successful tire deployments in New Jersey. Someone in the network of PEER members responded that they had an engineering report claiming concrete would melt underwater and release the tires. This was a ridiculous statement contrary to all known facts about concrete. I supplied an engineering report from a real engineer stating that concrete has no known lifespan. On top of that, fishery managers were recycling replaced concrete bridges by using them for artificial reefs.

I demanded to see a copy of the damming engineering report and when I backed them into a corner, they admitted they really didn't have a report, but observed concrete deteriorating underwater. I demanded to know where this deteriorating concrete was located, and they couldn't remember.

Next, there was the claim that nothing would grow on tires, the theory being that they emitted a poison that would kill marine life. Again, this was a false statement with no basis in scientific fact. Some people still use this false statement to discredit tires and now have

Reef Making

asserted a study by the European Commission's Plastics Strategy to support their claims. The study concluded that rubber in microscopic form was found on bridges and roadways near the water and was finding its way into the marine environment through runoff. Once in the marine environment, these particles were being ingested by marine animals and were suspected to be harmful. I agree with that study, but it doesn't apply to tires themselves.

Tires don't emit these particles unless they are ground off. The suspected harm caused by ground-up rubber was misapplied to tires rather than due to drainage problems from roadways and bridges. It's like saying fiberglass boats should be banned from the waterways because if you grind them up and ingest them, it could be harmful.

Unable to prove tire reefs were poisonous or structurally unsound, detractors turned to stability issues. They claimed the reef model was unstable and would move during storm events. Unknown to anyone but themselves, low-level Florida bureaucrats used tax dollars to hire a Miami engineering firm to conduct a "stability analysis" for "*Reefmaker* Tire Modules." The hope was that it would confirm the notion that my tire reefs were unstable and would move during storm events. The negative report would go to the Corps and that would be the end of it, or so they thought. Much to their regret, the six-page report stated: "The reef module would remain stable in a 50-year storm event." They kept this report hidden and continued to declare that my tire reefs were unstable. In fact, the report was never released to the Corps or the public and only turned up in my FOIA request.

Since I wasn't privy to the report, I supplied the formulas developed in New Jersey for weight-to-tire ratio and showed how I exceeded by 100 percent New Jersey's weight ratio of concrete to tire. Plus, I had a three-year track record of success. Of more than 3,000 reefs on the

New Reef Design and Florida

bottom, none moved. All Dr. Roberts wanted was to study 10 of my reefs for a period of years and if my claims proved to be untruthful, no more of them would be allowed and the reefs that were already in the water would be removed. Despite such assurances, none of this made any difference to all the bureaucrats who opposed tire reefs.

In the end, the Corps ignored all the facts, accepted the worst-case scenario of converting tires into reefs and never really considered permitting larger zones. The denied request for larger reef zones amounted to a big loss for fishermen in Florida and for any hope of environmentally sound-managed private reefs to increase fish stocks. It didn't end there either. Without permission, a low-level bureaucrat typing the Gulf States Marines Fisheries Commission protocol for reef material changed one word, "captured," into "embedded" after the former terminology had already been approved by the Commissioners. My reefs captured tires on concrete beams; the tires were not embedded in concrete. That word change effectively banned my tire reefs from every state except Alabama. Alabama refused to participate in the ruse and continued to approve the tire reef. To this day, 22 years after the first deployment, the tire reef is stable and working well. However, we no longer produce and deploy tire reefs, because we moved on to something better.

As the FOIA requests were coming in and I was sorting them in prosecutable order for my attorney, I got a call from someone whose name I won't mention. He suggested I build a different reef that didn't involve tires. He said if I did, my fortunes would change. I took the hint and adhered to the age-old saying: "If you can't beat 'em, join 'em." I eliminated the tires from the tetrahedron concrete frame and attached metal to it.

Reef Making

Steel reef.

Again, I got ideas from local fishermen such as Brian Annan. We got the metal from a table-cutting process. A large sheet of metal is placed on a table. A special machine cuts parts out of it. What is left is called a "skeleton." The skeletons were not free as were tires and I had to pay steel scrap value, plus trucking costs. Once delivered, the skeletons had to be welded together, cut into triangles and fastened onto the concrete tetrahedron frames. This drove the price up to $1,200 each.

Florida and other states immediately embraced the new reef and we deployed thousands as far away as the east coast of Florida to Texas. Eventually, we phased out the tire reef altogether. All the shortsighted individuals mentioned are no longer living or in power to influence decisions. I don't want to imply PEER itself was involved in any illegal or immoral activity. I have no evidence to implicate PEER itself; the problem came from some of their members using the membership rolls to conspire and collude with like-minded individuals against my reef. Thankfully, attitudes have changed, and the new generation of government employees assigned to projects that involve artificial reefs are responsible and reasonable people. I love to work with them, and I don't want to leave anyone with the impression that the hundreds of reef coordinators, scientists, marine biologists and others I've dealt with over the years were and are shortsighted and difficult. Only a handful of naysayers were involved in the tire reef debacle and for one reason or another all of them are no longer in positions of authority. Most of the people working with or associated with artificial reefs are dedicated and highly respected by those of us involved in artificial reef construction and deployment. I developed very good relationships with many of the old guard — relationships I treasure to this day.

CHAPTER 18

An Acceptable Reef

The evolution of artificial reefs occurred during the time of the land bubble in Orange Beach in the 1990s and for a few years beyond. In 2005 I lost my dock space again when the owner was offered more money for it than he could turn down. The owner walked away a rich man, but the developer eventually went bust due to all the other overpriced land deals of that time. In the meantime, though, we were booted out. Fortunately, I was able to purchase land on the ICW in Orange Beach, about a half-mile west of The Wharf, a large development next to the Foley Beach Express containing condos, a hotel, shops and restaurants. We quickly settled in and began the regular production of steel-clad reefs. A reporter from a Florida fishing magazine named our new reef design, "The Florida Special."

The same year both my sons, Stewart and Justin, came to work for me full-time. The three of us began to increase the quality and production rate of our reefs. There were other reef manufacturers, but none had the sort of cradle-to-grave operation as we did. We built our own molds, poured our own concrete and, using our own vessel, deployed the reefs up and down the Gulf Coast and beyond.

Reef Making

Now that we had a reef unit everybody liked, we began to expand our territory. We sold the reefs in Texas, Mississippi, Alabama and as far as the east coast of Florida. When I tried to sell them to Broward and Miami-Dade counties, I was turned down. The people I dealt with liked my reef, but explained that they only used boulders made from Florida limestone. I was told that it's the perfect reef material because the pH is perfect for all marine life and it's soft enough for the small boring animals at the bottom of the food chain to use it as their home sweet home. Bottom line, it couldn't be anything except Florida limestone.

I couldn't argue with them; it made perfect sense to me. I knew there was a concrete mix that offered a somewhat balanced pH, but no boring animals could live in concrete. Hence, Florida limestone was the perfect reef material and if I wanted the perfect reef, I would somehow need to find some to use. Our new location had a rock yard next door and it could supply us all the limestone we wanted. The problem was that their limestone came from north Alabama and was about 30 percent harder than Florida limestone. That was too hard for the tiny boring animals to bore. Compounding the problem was that regardless of where they fished, all my customers needed a big reef. A boulder big enough to satisfy the needs of a 30-passenger charter boat would weigh 50 tons.

As all this was going on, steel scrap prices were escalating. New laser machines were being sold that could cut more parts out of one sheet of metal. The metal spaces between the parts being cut were so small that it made the skeleton virtually worthless as reef material. We were down to one supplier that still used the old cutting method. Seeing the proverbial handwriting on the proverbial wall — that was all the motivation we needed to develop a better reef.

An Acceptable Reef

We put our heads together and came up with a different approach. What if we could use smaller rocks of Florida limestone and embed them in a concrete pyramid? The closest Florida limestone mine was in Marianna, between Pensacola and Tallahassee. I drove my pickup eastward through the Florida Panhandle and gathered a load of rocks. We began to experiment and, after more trial and error, managed to devise a way to build a pyramid with embedded rocks. It required a special mold and an unusual way of construction. Later, we discovered there are seven different types of Florida limestone. The Marianna rocks proved to be too soft and easily broke off from the reef. Finally, we found the perfect rock at another mine, but we had to truck it to Orange Beach, 25 tons at a time.

The new reef was pleasing to the eye and, more importantly, could support every marine animal that lives on a natural reef. A patent was obtained, and the new reef got a nice reception everywhere. It was so good, in fact, that people began to copy it and I began to spend a lot of time and money defending my patent in court.

CHAPTER 19

Complex Reef

As artificial reef building evolved, I heard more and more discussions about complex artificial reefs. It was at a point when everyone who manufactured artificial reefs, including me, produced a non-complex artificial reef. Basically, a complex artificial reef has small spaces for juvenile fish and small marine animals to gain shelter and protection from predators, just as a natural reef does. It was rare to see juvenile fish on a manufactured artificial reef because the concrete molding process made it impossible to cast spaces small enough to let little marine animals hide from predators.

The need for such a reef was far greater than anyone realized — and still is. Waterfront owners have hard-armored about 50 percent of the shorelines, in the process destroying estuaries that used to be there. The lack of estuary "nursing grounds" affects the biomass of fish and marine animals we are trying to increase and protect. There's not much we can do about developed shorelines now, but anything that protects juvenile fish leaving the estuary and moving offshore would be a great help. These juveniles are subject to becoming lunch for various adult species. If the biomass of younger fish was very large, it wouldn't make much difference, but the lack of estuary waters affects

Reef Making

the coastal food chain all the way up to the dinner table. If we intend to create artificial reefs as habitat for marine life, we need to mimic natural reefs to provide places for all marine life to live, not just the adult fish we like to eat. If we want more harvestable adults, we must make sure juveniles have the chance to mature. Part of that is protecting the juvenile fish leaving estuaries and moving offshore by providing a complex structure that affords them protection from predators along the way. Such shelters allow them to grow big enough to escape predation, and guarantee an increase in fish stocks.

So, I was on board with the notion of developing a complex artificial reef for all marine life to live, but I couldn't think of any way to modify my existing reef molds to fit the bill. Then I got a call from a resident of nearby Ono Island, Alabama. He was building a dock and wanted to install some artificial reefs under it. I predicted several problems with that. First, I didn't think he could obtain a Corps permit; also, the water was only 6 feet deep and my reef stood 8 feet tall. I would have to completely redesign my reef to fit.

I told the owner about the problems we faced, and said, "If you can obtain a permit, I will build you a reef." I figured I would never hear from him, because in modern times it takes years to obtain any kind of permit, and permits for artificial reefs are not issued to private individuals. However, the next day he called and said matter-of-factly, "I have the permit." I didn't know it, but the Corps had permits ready to issue for oyster reefs. He had asked for one and the agency handed it to him.

Then it was up to the *Reefmaker* crew to design a reef. We thought about cutting down our existing reef, but then decided to try to build a complex reef. I called my two sons together and explained the problem. I had a concept in mind and together we built an experimental

Complex Reef

mold. We made discs of concrete, with rocks in between. After we finished, the reef had several layers of a complex rock area between the layers of concrete. It weighed 6,000 pounds and we were worried it would sink into the sand underneath the customer's dock. We decided to mount it on a piling to elevate it above the bottom and see what happened. We wound up installing four units at no cost to the owner, providing he allowed free access to study how they fared. He agreed.

The new-fangled reefs were installed, and the dock was completed above it. Within six weeks, the reefs had about 40 mangrove snapper living on them, and the dock always seemed to have a cloud of baitfish around it. The reefs began to grow barnacles, soft corals, algae and oysters. Sheephead, crabs, shrimp, more mangrove snapper and other juvenile species began to show up.

After seeing the results, we were excited, but needed an easier way to manufacture the new design. It's funny how problems are sometimes solved. In this case, as we were standing at the reef and bouncing ideas around, a UPS truck pulled in. The driver joined our brainstorming circle, listened for a minute and asked nobody in particular, "Why don't you make them individually and stack them?" Bingo...his idea was what we were looking for. We tweaked the design into a stackable unit that could be mounted either on a piling or a pedestal.

We put some out in the Gulf of Mexico in 60 feet of water for study. Within a short while I was amazed to see hundreds of juvenile species using the reef, but almost no adults. Crabs, octopi and other species worked themselves into the cracks and crevices. It was doubtful the reef would appeal to our private reef customers, because they were interested in catching adult fish, so we introduced it to our customers in local and state government. We sold some to Mexico Beach (Florida) Artificial Reef Association. When the Florida Fish

First of Reefmaker's "Ecosystems" reefs

and Wildlife Conservation Commission's marine biologists dove on them, they were excited by the number of juvenile fish and began to recommend this type of reef at conferences. We named the new reef unit "EcoSystems." Each disc is 12 inches tall and four feet in diameter, with a 10-inch hole in the center. The discs can be stacked on a 10-inch piling or a concrete disc pedestal. The height of the reef can be increased to any desired height by adding more discs. The stackable design also has unlimited possibilities for different reef shapes.

Following up on some advice from Dr. Bill Lindberg of the University of Florida, we later developed a grouper reef module. Lindberg is the leading expert on gag grouper, which like caves and shallow ledges. They will even dig sand from under a ledge to build a home. To make them feel welcome in our reef, we modified an old septic tank mold with one side cut out. The box was only a couple of feet tall and provided little relief from the bottom, so we added an EcoSystems reef

Complex Reef

EcoSystems reef

to the top and it likewise became a very popular reef. The EcoSystems' design allows it to be added as an option to our existing pyramids to add complexity.

This was exciting work; no more dumping old cars and buses. A progression of ideas based on what fish and fishermen needed and what we could provide was at work in those years. Alas, that was then, and this is now. Artificial reef designs have remained somewhat stagnant when it comes to technological advances. Todd Barber of Reef-

Reef Making

Grouper reef with EcoSystems on top

Ball and myself have had many discussions concerning this. With all this advanced reef technology available, one would think government officials in charge of artificial reef programs in their respective states would jump onboard and start planning designer reefs. Unfortunately, most seem at the mercy of "that's-the-way-we've-always-done-it" syndrome. Bridge rubble, old concrete culverts and other concrete debris are collected, stored, prepared, trucked to staging locations, loaded on barges, transported offshore and deployed. As the concrete is pushed over the side of the barge, it lands in haphazard arrays on the bottom. The inherent weight of concrete assures it will subside into the bottom a bit. Unless carefully stacked, it doesn't provide much relief off the bottom or much complexity. We've found that the bottom 12 inches of a reef supports very little life due to the sandblast effect and silt. The upper parts of a reef are the most productive. Compared to a tall structure, concrete rubble rarely provides enough relief to support the quantity and quality of marine life that makes it worth the trouble.

Few consider the years of embedded contamination of dripped oil, grease, chemicals and antifreeze from hundreds of thousands of automobiles on bridge rubble, much less the various chemicals that concrete culverts might have been exposed to. Economically, once you add all the costs associated with the collection, preparation, transport and deployment of concrete debris it pales in comparison to a manufactured reef. A manufactured reef of greater size, height and complexity deployed in a planned pattern benefits the fishery by a factor of 10 and can be had for the same cost. Yet when I attempt to convey this message, I always get the same answer: "We get the concrete for free."

Junk and concrete rubble continue to be deployed with little or no thought regarding how the reef might protect juvenile fish, increase

Grouper reef with EcoSystems

different species of marine life, improve substrate PH, accommodate natural reef animals and strengthen the food chain in general. It's a shame funding for such a study can't be included among the many grants given to marine scientists.

We have the technology to design reefs that serve a specific need and impact different target species and age groups needing a boost in their biomass to balance the fishery. There is still much to be learned.

Until recently, all efforts to convey this idea have fallen on deaf ears. This message has received favorable reaction to the ears and minds of some reef coordinators, including the Mexico Beach Artificial Reef Association and others, who have begun to group different types of reefs together to provide habitat for all species and marine life age groups.

We are starting to see more experimental designs suggested by our customers. For instance, Alabama requested a design change to our pyramid to compartmentalize the structure with compartments of varying sizes to accommodate fish and marine animals of different sizes better. Hopefully the tide is turning, and officials are beginning to see the long-term advantages of creating artificial reefs with the goal of managing the fishery from estuary to dinner plate.

CHAPTER 20

Snorkeling Reef

We wondered if the EcoSystem pile mounted reef would survive a hurricane. A perfect laboratory for that purpose became available in 2007. My friend Harold Sherman was building the new Gulf State Park Fishing Pier at Gulf Shores to replace the old one destroyed during Hurricane Ivan. We thought placing our reefs in the surf next to the beach would be the ultimate test. Harold was agreeable and he got permission to install a couple of EcoSystems units on pilings next to the pier. They stayed there for a year and endured three storm events with no damage, even when 19 of the new pier's 2.5-foot by 2.5-foot concrete pilings broke during one of the storms.

Our experiments with a pile-mounted reef attracted the attention of Robert Turpin, the Escambia County Reef Coordinator in Pensacola. He asked if we could install the reef on pilings close to the beach so they might become a snorkeling reef for access to beachgoers. I answered in the affirmative, even though I didn't have a clue of how I was going to install it. Robert was able to obtain a Corps permit and we set about designing and building tools to install it. In 2011, we

Testing of EcoSystems units.

installed the first-ever EcoSystems snorkeling reef at Pensacola Beach. It consisted of 38 pile-mounted units, 3 discs per unit.

    We applied for and obtained a patent for the reef and it became a major attraction at Pensacola Beach for snorkelers, scuba divers, kayakers and beach fishermen. It was so popular that the word spread quickly and more permits were obtained. In Florida, Perdido Key and Navarre, plus Walton, Santa Rosa and Okaloosa counties placed orders. Alabama followed suit. All who installed the snorkeling reef reported increases in tourism. Alabama was sold on the benefits as well and installed several. The beauty of this design is that it solves a problem associated with shallow-water reefs. Normally, they would tend to subside due to wave action and soon disappear under the sand or else be carried away by current. Mounting such a reef on a piling that supports the weight is the solution. We usually install them seven feet underwater adjacent to a beach for snorkelers. However, in Mexico Beach, we installed some in 30 feet of water for fishing purposes. In 2018, those units survived completely intact after destructive category 5 Hurricane Michael slammed into Mexico Beach.

Deploying the reef close to a beach poses the biggest problem. Operating a vessel in the surf zone requires a very good weather day with seas of less than 1 foot. Plus, installing a reef on a piling typically involves lots of dive time, further complicating the mission. One-foot sea days are few and far apart, so we needed to be able to deploy as quickly as possible. Putting our heads together, we developed a deployment method that wasn't dependent on the use of divers and were able to deploy 38 units in one day.

That's quite a feat considering the nail-biting deployment involved. The vessel is held in position by spuds, which are steel beams that travel through tubes in the barge. They come to rest on the sea floor

Snorkeling reefs off Pensacola Beach

Reef Making

Installing snorkeling reefs.

and hold the barge in place. These work well if sea conditions are optimum. But even the slightest swell will lift a 600-ton barge slightly and thrust it toward the beach, putting hundreds of tons of bending force on the spuds. If the steel spud bends under such a tremendous load, the barge is trapped in place. The spud can't be pulled up through its tube thru the deck of the barge. Likewise, it can't be cut off without divers doing the work. Such scenarios always seem to be a threat as the weather worsens. It's a horrible situation and a constant concern for anyone using this method of deployment.

Snorkeling Reef

Even so, the business the snorkel reefs generated was too good to pass up. As we began to sell more and more snorkel reefs, our customers requested deployment patterns in the shape of turtles, seahorses, fish, dolphins, starfish and others. All these patterns were designed to be seen from space via satellites.

At any rate, deploying a snorkel reef was a daunting task requiring pinpoint accuracy. It required a much more stable platform and a much more sophisticated GPS. Such equipment isn't available in the open marketplace and had to be designed and built expressly for us. We purchased a "jackup vessel" and attached our own specially designed GPS equipment to the crane. We also acquired an installation tool of our own design to make the process faster and more efficient.

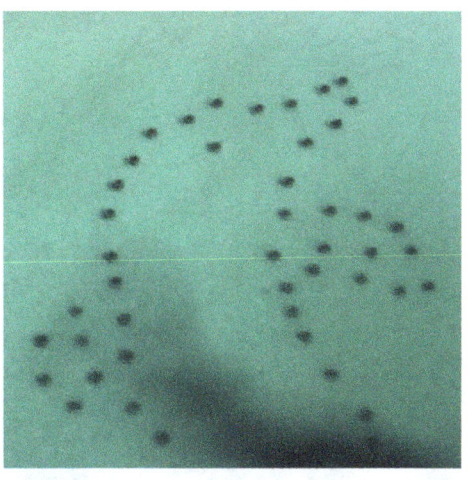

Walton County's EcoSystems snorkeling reefs.

Over the years, we perfected the deployment procedure. The jackup boat is loaded each day and travels from protected water to the deployment site. It elevates above the water and employs two cranes — one to install the reef and the other to assemble the next reef for deployment. We have installed hundreds of reefs using this method.

Reef Making

Aerial view of snorkel reef

CHAPTER 21

Super Reef

Not long ago, Alabama officials asked if we could build a very large reef (25 feet tall) to mimic the size of a ship. Their thinking was that the reefs could be deployed next to each other to create a very large reef. The main problem facing anyone manufacturing a large reef is the weight and how to handle it. For example, an 8-foot-tall pyramid reef weighs three tons, but a 15-foot-tall pyramid reef weighs 18 tons. The extra weight of what we called a "Super Reef" 25 feet tall would exceed the capacity of the *Maranatha* and its crane. Thus, tackling a reef the size the Alabama officials wanted would require the purchase of a large barge and crane to handle the extra weight. Even so, we bid on the job and won it. We went looking for a suitable barge and crane and found a 170-foot by 39-foot barge and a 110-ton (capacity) crane in Louisiana.

The *Maranatha* then went to Louisiana to pick up the barge and crane as we began to build new molds for the 18-ton monster-size reef. We didn't have a crane in the yard large enough to handle the new reef so we arranged the molds close to the water, which would allow the new barge crane access to the production area. It could assist in lifting the parts into their proper positions and then the completed reef. Large-capacity release hooks and super-size lifting lines all had to be sized, built and tested. Later we purchased a 60-ton crane to assemble the reefs, but left the heavy lifting to the barge crane.

The *Maranatha* is designed with push knees and winches for handling barges, and it was able to mate up to the barge and attach itself for the reef deployment trip. We were fortunate that Dan Baird, a tug captain with 60 years of experience, was there to help us. Dan started on tugboats when they were wooden, underpowered, single-engine boats. Tugs have two methods of handling barges: Pushing from behind or towing. Pushing requires the tug to fasten itself to the barge with winches and heavy cables tight enough to make it and the barge one unit. The other method is towing via single line from the front of the barge.

Pushing gives the tugboat total control over the barge. Towing puts the barge at the mercy of wind and current and only the best of captains like Dan can control it inside canals, channels and rivers. However, pushing a barge in any kind of wind or current requires a lot of horsepower from twin engines to force the barge to do the will of the captains. Even then there are limits. Believe it or not, a loaded barge is easier to control than an empty barge. Tug crews sometimes can be seen tying up empty barges to canal banks in times of high winds to wait for the blustery weather to calm down.

In the old days of single-engine, low-horsepower tugs, skippers were forced to tow barges just about everywhere. This is where the artful skill of towing barges was developed. To watch Dan work a tugboat and barge is a pure delight. Dan doesn't rely on horsepower, but rather he uses the wind and current to do his work. I can't recall ever hearing Dan accelerate the engines much over idle until he was underway.

Super Reef

There's a funny story he told on himself regarding an early trip he made on a twin-engine tug. This occurred right after twin-engine tugs first appeared. The new models had two main engines and two generator sets. It was customary that every 24 hours the crew would switch generators to service the one that was used the previous 24 hours. On this particular trip Dan and his deckhand transferred from an old single-engine tug they were familiar with to a new twin-engine boat attached to a large fuel barge they were supposed to deliver 200 miles away. They had been on the boat for a couple of days when Dan got a call from the owner on the radio. He was complaining about Dan's tardiness. Dan said, "I've got it at full throttle and doing the best it can." The owner told him that the previous captain made the same trip in a lot less time. It seems that Dan was only using one engine at a time. He didn't know he was supposed to use them both. He would shut one down as he would the generator sets. Dan even docked, undocked, and shifted barges on one engine.

Dan was an excellent captain by any measure. We needed his skills, because getting the barge to the exact location for a reef deployment required good control. Not that it was impossible to position the barge using a towline configuration, but it would take a lot of extra time. Imagine threading a needle holding the thread 12 inches from the end of the thread. Pushing the barge to the spot wasn't nearly as complicated.

There was another problem with pushing that we had to contend with, though. Pushing can only be done in calm weather. Assume you're dealing with two vessels weighing hundreds of tons tied together with cables. If a swell rolls a vessel one way the second vessel is likely to go in another direction and they pull at each other. Then cables might snap and the two vessels separate in a precarious posi-

Reef Making

Super reefs.

tion, still connected by some cables. The remainder of the cables must be removed, and a towline attached to the barge, all without injuring crewman or killing them in a pitching sea. Another scenario is an empty barge caught by the wind and sailing away quickly. Chasing it down with a tug might be problematic because some barges can sail faster than a tug can go. To avoid this, we limited our deployment days to when there were 1-foot seas.

Any swell produced a rolling motion in the barge. The crane had an 800-pound block and hook that would become uncontrollable as it swung back and forth, even with an expert crane operator. The men on the barge had to catch this block and stop it from swinging long enough to hook it to the reef. Imagine a 150-pound man trying to stop an 800-pound block as it comes swinging by at 20 mph. We struggled through several years doing what we could, until orders for the Super Reefs became more than the number of 1-foot sea days we could count on.

Super Reef

We needed a vessel like the *Maranatha* that could handle the Super Reefs and a rougher sea as well. It would require a much larger vessel able to deploy reefs in 3- to 4-foot seas. We looked at a lot of options, but decided on an offshore supply vessel. There were plenty tied up and idle in Louisiana because the oil field economy collapsed again. What would be ideal, we thought, was one with Dynamic Positioning (DP), which is a computer that takes control of the engines and bow thruster to hold the vessel in one position without it moving, regardless of wind and current.

Most of the vessels we looked at had been neglected. Some had been robbed of serviceable parts and refitted with worn-out parts by owners trying to keep at least one vessel of their fleet running. We found one that might have been the oldest of the fleet, but it was in the best condition. That's not to say it was in great condition, but it passed muster. Though it had no DP, we could buy the boat, install a new DP and add a used 85-ton-capacity oil platform crane for a reasonable price.

Installation of the crane and DP took almost a year. As we spent time inside our new vessel, we found a lot of things that needed repair. During the year of refitting the new vessel, our main concern was fuel consumption. The *Maranatha* generated 800 hp and consumed 30 gallons per hour (gph) at eight knots. The new vessel had 3,000 hp and we were told to expect 75 gph at top speed of 12 knots. We were very pleased to find that if we ran it at reduced speed, we could get 35 gph at nine knots. I must give the glory to God for this vessel. We named her the *Maranatha II*.

No one had ever installed a Seatrax crane on a supply boat. It was a big crane and its weight and height above the deck constituted a "center-of-gravity" concern. Add to that the 250 tons of reefs — all of

Reef Making

Marantha II *super reef deployment.*

which stood taller than any load the boat was designed for — and we wondered if it would turn over.

Calculating the center of gravity with the crane and 12 Super Reefs was beyond my mathematical skills. The only way I could be sure the vessel was safe to operate was to test it. We decided to do that at the dock; if it turned over in 10 feet of water, it would limit the salvage cost and avoid any deaths. We loaded a dozen Super Reefs onboard, then picked up a Super Reef and swung it over the side as if deploying it. We made sure all the watertight doors were secured to decrease water entry into the vessel if it rolled over. Carefully we inched the reef over the side, keeping it close to the vessel. So far, so good. We lowered the reef into the water near the bottom and slowly boomed out until it was a good distance away from the vessel. We lifted the reef out the water and although the boat leaned precariously, it was rock-solid and passed the test. At this writing the *Maranatha II* has deployed a couple of hundred Super Reefs in various sea conditions with no problems.

Watching the vessel work is a marvel to behold. My son Stewart pilots the vessel to the deployment location and finds what he calls a "sweet spot," meaning to position the bow in a direction that minimizes the rolling action. At this point, he engages the Dynamic Positioning system. It takes control of the two main engines, the bow thruster and the rudders. It calculates wind speed and direction, current direction and speed and wave height. Engines rev up, followed by great foamy eruptions from all three propellers. Within a few minutes, the vessel settles down in a rock-solid position with the bow facing any direction we choose. The DP holds the vessel perfectly still. Using the survey grade GPS unit attached to the crane boom, one reef after another can be deployed in very close proximity to each other and in any pattern desired by our customer. If the vessel needs to move slightly, it has a joystick that will move the vessel in any direction and/or heading.

This truly is a state-of-the-art reef deployment vessel and makes its predecessors obsolete. Soon the *Maranatha* tug, barge and crane will be phased out of service altogether.

CHAPTER 22

Turtles

In 2010, the infamous BP Deepwater Horizon oil spill occurred in the Gulf of Mexico south of Louisiana and Mississippi. The disaster ultimately led to billions of dollars in fines being distributed to Gulf states in part to mitigate the ecological nightmare that ensued. In 2015, some of the money BP was fined due to the oil spill was seeping into state coffers for the building of artificial reefs.

I got a phone call from Texas officials inquiring about reef modules whose construction and deployment would be paid for with some of the BP funds that were being released to their reef program. Since such funds are routed through the federal government, NOAA got a say in the process. NOAA stopped Texas' purchase of artificial reefs until it was proven a turtle could escape if somehow trapped inside the artificial reef. When they get sleepy, turtles wedge themselves under something for a nap that might last as long as 20 minutes. When they wake up, they head for the surface for a breath of air. For some inexplicable reason, they swim straight up without regard of their surroundings. If "up" is blocked, they panic and instead of returning the way they came to escape, they die. Turtles die in caves, shipwrecks and sometimes, but rarely artificial reefs. Our reef units

Reef Making

were designed so there is no place for a turtle to get inside, either from underneath or through the "windows," which are too small. However, one reef we deployed a few years ago landed on the toe of another and it tilted the reef enough to accommodate a turtle under it. This was before we were using the new GPS system.

In 2009, Will Paterson, a research scientist, found skeletal remains of a turtle in this reef. It was alleged by NOAA that the turtle woke up from a nap and instead of backing out, it went farther in and then up, only to find no escape. Consequently, it died. No thought was given to the notion that perhaps the turtle had been wounded by a predator, sought refuge in the reef and died there, or that it simply died a natural death. None of this was considered and NOAA would not allow the project to go forward until the issue was addressed to its satisfaction.

No one — especially me — wants to build something that might kill a turtle. I was very concerned. I called NOAA and asked to speak to the turtle expert who issued the decree about escape holes. I was forwarded to the individual and I explained who I was, and told him of my concern. I asked if he could help me with the dimensions of the hole for the turtles to escape through. To my surprise, he told me he wouldn't supply me with that information, and he wouldn't approve the reef until I could prove it was turtle-safe. It wasn't that NOAA didn't know the proper size, because this is the same agency that required all shrimp nets have a turtle excluder device with precise dimensions for the escape hole.

I tried to find someone else at NOAA who could supply me with the information I needed, all to no avail. Another issue I needed to resolve related to the shape of the "escape hole." Because of the pyramidal design of my reef, it made sense that the escape hole would be triangular-shaped, instead of square like the shrimp net hole. Any suggested dimensions or designs I offered were rejected. Frustrated, I went online and purchased a plastic rendition of an adult loggerhead turtle, which is the biggest turtle in the Gulf. We cut one side of the reef down for a triangular hole large enough for two turtles to fit with flippers extended. I took a photo of my son holding the plastic turtle and standing next to the hole and sent it the NOAA expert. He didn't have any choice except to approve the reef. In an aside, he told me he would provide no documentation affirming that we met their requirements because he hated artificial reefs and wished there were none out there.

His objection to artificial reefs had no scientific basis. If he were really concerned about the health of the turtle population, he would cheer us on to make more artificial reefs. Artificial reefs aren't any

Turtle escape opening

Reef Making

more harmful to turtles than natural reefs. In fact, quite the opposite is true. According to the Sea Turtle Conservancy "Sea turtles typically spend their juvenile years eating and growing in nearshore habitats" (Natural & artificial reefs). "Once they reach adulthood and sexual maturity, it is believed that they migrate to a new feeding ground." Since we have no natural habitat here in the northern Gulf of Mexico, it's a fair assumption that artificial habitat is providing food and protection for turtles. There is plenty of evidence to support this theory. Just ask any diver.

About two years after all this took place, another turtle expert from NOAA wrote a "memo" requiring a 48-inch hole in all artificial reefs for turtle escape. As I noted before, my hole is triangular and would have to be enlarged to meet the 48-inch square opening. Turtle expert No. 2 completely ignored the photo of the adult loggerhead turtle in the opening of my reef, which was large enough for two turtles to exit at the same time if need be.

The NOAA gentleman spoke at a reef conference and I asked to meet with him. I showed him the picture of the turtle in the hole. He said he couldn't approve my reef because the hole was triangular-shaped, thus it wouldn't meet the 48-inch-square recommendation. I asked him why NOAA couldn't determine the size of a triangular opening that would work for a turtle. After all, they did the same for TEDs (Turtle Excluder Devices). He stated NOAA only hires marine biologists and had no engineers. Likewise, they couldn't afford to hire an engineering firm to determine the hole required. Of course, in the practical world where most of us live none of this made sense, except to NOAA.

Before I left for the conference, I researched the Code of Federal Regulations (CFRs) for shrimp net turtle excluder device requirements. They indicated a 40-inch opening. I showed the NOAA guy a copy of the CFR. His response was that the regulation was no longer valid. However — and I will give him credit for this — the next day he emailed me, apologized and admitted it was indeed a valid regulation. Consequently, it threw a monkey wrench into his 48-inch requirement. He stated he would have to review his recommendation and get back to me. So far, all's been quiet. However, the Florida-based Corps of Engineers tried to write the 48-inch opening into all new reef-permitted sites based on his no-longer-valid memo. I sent the Corps copies of my correspondence with the NOAA turtle guy and they backed off. Now all our reefs either have a turtle escape hole more than large enough or the design nullifies the need for one. After the initial problem, to date no dead turtles have been found in our reefs.

CHAPTER 23

Wave Attenuator

As we continued to study the dock reef, it occurred to us that we should try to use it for a wave attenuator to help keep shorelines from washing away. Bulkheads destroy any estuary value of the shoreline. A wave attenuator installed a distance offshore from the shoreline would protect it from erosion and allow grassy estuary to grow in the shallow water on or next to the shoreline.

We thought the complex design might destroy wave energy without stopping the water from passing through. If wave attenuators are designed heavy enough to stay in place during storm events, it means that over time they're likely to subside and become useless. Too light and they'll move during storm events. The other problem is blocking the free flow of water. This causes stagnant water to accumulate behind it.

Small, lightweight wave attenuators are not tall enough to work if the tide rises, as it always does during storms. The waves go over them and erode the shoreline. Likewise, they can't withstand heavy pounding of waves and are torn from their positions and moved into deeper water or channels. They wind up causing hazards to navigation, foul-

Reef Making

ing fishing nets and damaging grassy estuaries. Piling supports our system, so it can't sink or move. Its patented design doesn't interfere with the free flow of water, but only dissipates the wave energy. Our EcoSystems not only solve all the problems associated with other wave attenuators, it also provides a complex reef habitat for marine life exiting the estuary it protects. Aquatic grass can be planted successfully behind it, even where none existed before.

We tested the reef unit on a fiberglass piling in the surf of the Gulf of Mexico for one year, during which there were three major storm events. We also installed a couple next to our dock in Orange Beach and began to play with the design. Coincidentally, we got a call from Heather Reed, the project manager in charge of overseeing the protection of Deadman's Island for the city of Gulf Breeze. Deadman's Island is a historic site on the east side of Pensacola Bay that was eroding and exposing coffins from an old graveyard. It needed to be protected, without destroying the beach. Oyster baskets were tried, but they were too small and the waves went over them. We agreed to install some of our units at cost to study how effective they were. They worked at dissipating the waves and provided a lot of habitat for marine life.

Next, we installed 1,000 feet at the Yellow River Marsh Preserve in Milton, Florida. Local landowners were losing 20 feet of shoreline each year. EcoSystems stopped the loss and word spread. I got a call from Darrell Westmoreland and Randy Boyd of North State Environmental about developing a system for the Cape Fear River in North Carolina. The problem there involved ship wakes eroding the riverbanks. The feeling was that our wave attenuator would meet all their needs. I set North State Environmental up as a licensee and a test section was installed. So far, the tests have all been successful.

Yellow River Marsh Preserve with Reefmaker's wave attenuator.

In addition, Ecosystems was chosen over all the other available wave attenuator products for a mitigation project concerning the Bonner Bridge in North Carolina. We are continually enhancing the design and I see a bright future for this product.

CHAPTER 24

The Future and Restoring the World's Fisheries

It's taken many years, but the long-term benefits of artificial reefs, both economic and environmental, are beginning to receive attention and acknowledgment from bureaucrats, the media and the non-fishing public. Two comprehensive studies were conducted in Florida on the economic impact of artificial reefs to local economies. Each study found that for every dollar spent on an artificial reef, a positive impact of $131 was added to the local economy. Seemingly a no-brainer; one would think such positive economic news would spur local politicians to push for more artificial reefs. The benefits include job creation, growth and increases to the tax base. Sadly, many politicians seem geared more toward general voter approval and not toward sound business practices. They would rather spend money on a park whose maintenance would have a negative impact on funds, be less beneficial and serve fewer people. On the other hand, an artificial reef would provide an astronomical return of a $131-to-$1 ratio in economic value, with no maintenance needed. As proven, a robust reef system attracts tourist fishermen, serves locals and helps hotels,

Reef Making

restaurants and shops prosper while providing an increase in tax revenues far exceeding any other type of public project.

If we can't get politicians involved, we have a willing group of fishermen ready to invest millions in a private reef program. It's a shame that Alabama is the only state to embrace the concept. Alabama's leaders see the value of a private reef program that costs the government nothing, but still returns $131 to the local economy for every dollar spent. The downside — or at least an issue that must be addressed and resolved — is that the money invested by private fishermen is directly proportional to the amount of fish they can harvest. Here is a fish-farming program that is increasing the biomass of red snapper and is fully paid for by individual fishermen. Yet their access to the benefits is restricted by government regulations that are, at times, heavy-handed and unfair. It's like asking a farmer to spend the money and provide the labor to plant a crop. Then, when the time of harvest comes, the government won't allow the farmer access under penalty of fines and/or arrest.

Some change is in the wind. Alabama officials are still leading the way with their investment in artificial reefs. They are permitting new reef areas inside bays and sounds and within nine miles of the beach. These officials are spending millions of dollars from the Deepwater Horizon BP Oil Spill settlement money on artificial reefs. Northwest Florida and Texas are doing the same. Mississippi is spending BP money on beach or shoreline protection projects, though not on artificial reefs. Who knows what happened to the money given to Louisiana, as very little has been spent on artificial reefs?

Science is slowly increasing knowledge of the effects of artificial reefs on the marine environment and the interaction of marine life on those structures. Through the efforts of researchers, organizations, reef manufacturers and local officials in charge of reef deployments, real progress is being made. The biggest problem is the limited funds and the short-term study periods that limited funds mandate. However, even local groups such as Mexico Beach Artificial Reef Association maintain a constant and comprehensive study of their reef program, thanks to the volunteer efforts of folks like Bob and Carol Cox. They've teamed with a medical research facility to collect samples of marine life found on their artificial reefs for possible curative value. Their in-depth study of artificial reefs includes their careful recording (supported by photos and scientific names) of all observed marine life. Such data provide more insight into how each artificial reef works. The effects of complex over non-complex reefs, the interaction of complex and non-complex reefs and how "big" reefs relate to "little" reefs are important elements to study. Likewise, questions remain regarding how marine life relates to reefs in shallow water and deep water, and how different types of reefs might be grouped together for best results. All this knowledge is being accumulated and cataloged. This information has been extremely valuable and beneficial to reef designers who avail themselves of it.

Bob and Carol aren't the only ones collecting data and working tirelessly to further artificial reefs. Robert Turpin, Escambia County's reef coordinator; Alex Fogg, Okaloosa County's reef coordinator; Andy McAlexander of the South Walton Artificial Reef Association; Keith Millie of FWC; Melinda Gates of Walton County, Alan Golden of Bay County; Alan Richardson of OAR; Chris Blankenship, Scott Bannon, Craig Newton, and Kevin Anson of the Alabama Department of Conservation and Natural Resources; Dale Shively and Dr. Brooke Shipley of the Texas Parks and Recreation; plus others too numerous to list here have worked tirelessly to procure and deploy reefs for the benefit of both fishermen and the health of the fishery.

As the value of reefs becomes more apparent, "new" uses have moved apace with projects to understand their value to marine life. For instance, the sport of snorkeling reefs is gaining traction — especially in Northwest Florida. Governmental bodies in Alabama and the Florida Panhandle recognize the economic benefits of recreational snorkeling and support it. The first snorkeling reef we installed was at Pensacola Beach, deployed in 2014, and it was such a success that other counties began clamoring for their own. Farther east at Navarre, the locals have seen a large increase in tourist spending due to their investment in snorkeling reefs. Convinced by the results generated by the first one, they've increased the size of their snorkeling reef system. I foresee an increase in these types of reefs worldwide and we are working on some interesting new snorkeling reef designs.

I envision seaside resorts with snorkeling reef playgrounds and art parks. Not only will they prove entertaining for tourists, but they serve an educational purpose by putting a wide range of sea life in its natural habitat on display. Developing these new reefs for maximum benefit is a challenging undertaking, presenting a wide range of problems in the design and installation. Even so, we have some great ideas and designs for release very soon.

Environmentally friendly wave attenuators are beginning to be recognized as beneficial to the marine environment. Finally, the Corps of Engineers has recognized that hard-armoring shorelines with rocks and bulkheads are destroying our nation's estuaries. We have lost over 50 percent of our private shoreline/estuary due to bulkheading. Our EcoSystems wave attenuator not only protects the shoreline from erosion, it accommodates a grassy estuary behind it, providing more

The Future and Restoring the World's Fisheries

habitat for marine life. Oysters love the natural limestone rock, and juvenile marine life finds protection in its complex design. It can withstand storm events in places no other manufactured wave attenuator could.

So far it has proven extremely successful in bays, rivers and sounds. We are getting more requests for it to take on ocean waves. This is a daunting task, but our engineers have designed a structure that can hold up in this environment. We hope to test it soon in the Bahamas.

Artificial reefs have the capability to solve most of the world's fishery problems. Most third-world countries are experiencing problems with their fisheries. Overfishing and harsh harvesting methods are destroying the fisheries' capacity to feed their countries' human inhabitants. It's frustrating to know we have a wealth of knowledge here in Alabama to help third-world countries restore their fisheries and increase their production. All it would require is a little education and some governmental cooperation. Training fishermen to farm fish instead of overharvesting them is the answer. Once we show fishermen the benefits of managing their own personal reefs in a sustainable fashion, it will open their eyes. Eventually, the tremendous economic benefits that resulted would help fishermen and their families everywhere lift themselves out of poverty. It's my heartfelt desire that we're enabled to share what we know with the rest of the world to make it happen.

We are partnering with marine environment think tanks to find ways to increase oyster production, overcome problems with invasive species and improve water quality.

As of this writing, I am 73 years old. My stepson, Justin, left reef building and became a nurse. I always encouraged my children to find something they enjoy and then find a way to make a living at it.

Reef Making

Although I'm sad he's not still part of Walter Marine, he's very good at what he does, and I am very proud of his accomplishments.

My son, Stewart, is my right hand. He's taken to reef building as I did, and I couldn't operate without him. I am amazed by his abilities. Many businesses passed down to sons tend to fail. I am confident this business will continue on in the traditions and principled ways we've followed since 1968. I see Stewart at the reins when I'm not able to go on anymore. God has blessed me beyond what I could ever have hoped for and dreamt. I owe everything to Him. As I look out my office window and reflect on the past, I know I never would have dreamed that those small beginnings so many years ago would have resulted in a reef manufacturing facility of the size it is today. To date, Reefmaker has deployed over 45,000 artificial reefs and still counting.

I give God all the glory and I know it would not be so without Him.

www.ingramcontent.com/pod-product-compliance
Lightning Source LLC
Chambersburg PA
CBHW070800040426
42333CB00060B/1229